I DARE YA!

I DARE YA!

ANDREW STANLEY
& DAMIAN CLARK

MERLIN
PUBLISHING

First published in 2008 by
Merlin Publishing
Newmarket Hall, Cork Street,
Dublin 8, Ireland
Tel: +353 1 4535866
Fax: +353 1 4535930
publishing@merlin.ie
www.merlinwolfhound.com

13-Digit ISBN 978-1-903582-87-9

A CIP catalogue record for this book is available from the British Library.

10 9 8 7 6 5 4 3 2 1

Cover Design & Typesetting by Artwerk
Cover image courtesy of Damian Clark
Printed and bound by CPI Cox & Wyman, Britain

CONTENTS

ACKNOWLEDGEMENTS

Many thanks to Jean & the Animo team, Ray Darcy, Edcom6, all at Lisa Richards, Aoife Flynn, Merlin (not the wizard), Anita Corcoran, everyone at the International Bar, the Laughter Lounge gang, lovely Sandra, and all you darers and your warped imaginations.

Oh and Mexican Food - A & D

MEET THE AUTHORS

ANDREW

Name: Andrew W. Stanley

Born: 12th July 1980

King William of Orange day. Figured out what the middle initial stands for yet?

Birth place: Swords, Co Dublin. Not really Dublin. Not really not Dublin.

Hair: Brown. Not red! Brown.

Eyes: Blue

Likes: Biscuits, music, TV, films, crisps, Subway sandwiches

Dislikes: Quiznos subs, crackers

One thing to do before you die: Write a book. Oh wait...

DAMO

Name: Damian J. Clark.
'Damo' to my mates and 'Get away from me' to the ladies.

Born: 18th November 1977

Just after *The Omen* was released in cinemas and my parents thought 'Damian's a nice name'.

Birth place: Adelaide, Australia.

Hair: Fair with bald highlights

Eyes: Poo brown

Likes: Watching cartoons, hearing aluminium cans open, bike rides at night and rock!

Dislikes: TV license inspectors and clampers

One thing to do before you die: Fly a rocket pack. C'mon NASA!! We know you have them!!!

THE
I DARE YA!
STORY!!
(so far...)

After a stand-up gig in Portlaoise, Andrew and Damo were kickin' back, having a laugh. As you do, they began daring each other to do stuff…

…which they followed through.

It was exciting!

On the train to Dublin the next morning...

...the lads had an idea.

At their next gig, they began asking the audience for dares and then carried them out.

This was fun so the boys took the dare show to the Edinburgh Fringe Festival.

The crowds enjoyed it and so did Andrew and Damo.

On returning to Ireland they received a chance to do the exact same thing on telly.

After the series was broadcast, they both toured around the country to more audiences and doing more dares.

With over 200 dares done and thousands of dares collected, you now hold the compilation of the best and the craziest. Enjoy!

INTRO

Welcome to I Dare Ya, *the book where you, the reader, have written most of the content. Andrew Stanley and Damian Clark (that's us) set out in 2007 to become the nation's monkey boys and as a result, performed a number of silly dares and stunts to the amusement of the Irish public.*

We have now decided to reminisce about these in book form and also include some of the best dares that were considered for addition but unfortunately we haven't had a chance to do...yet. So have a read and see what ya think about dares from all across the nation and beyond and whether or not you could have sent in a better one.

I DARE YA!

EAT, DRINK & BE CRAZY

Spewing is gross. But it's also hilarious!! All the words to describe spew are funny: puke, barf, hurl, chuck, sick, vomit, chunder, regurgitate, technicolour yawn, liquid belch, the list goes on.
Why are we mentioning this?

If you try some of these dares and you don't die or get your head kicked in, spewing is option #3.

EAT

Location: swimming pool.
Put a melted Star Bar in the water and pretend it's a poo. Then pick it up and eat it in front of the other swimmers.
Mazz, Kilkenny

Eat a whole lizard without chewing.
Katie, Dublin

A: Thank God I'm vegetarian!

Eat 1,000 packets of Jelly Babies.
Max, Dublin

Join Weight Watchers and bring a big bag of snacks!
Rose & JP, Cork

I dare ya to go into an O'Briens Irish Sandwich Bar and pretend you are friends with Brody Sweeney (the man who started the first shop). Say that he sent you down to try a free sandwich because you're interested in opening a shop abroad. Even better if you get a free drink too!!
Jackie, Meath

Eat loads of food and then make yourself sick on your t-shirt and go round wearing the t-shirt in town.
Keith, Meath

See how fast you can eat a litre tub of ice-cream.
Colm

Put some ketchup on a sausage and stick it in someone's ear and tell them not to ring the Gardaí.
Eoghan, Tallaght

Find a huge lawn with a 'keep off the grass' sign and set up a picnic beside the sign.
John, Kilkenny

Eat as many raw potatoes as possible.
Ciaran, Cavan

DRINK

I dare ya to drink 100 beers (bottles or cans) over 72 hours.
Stra & Diggs

A: I am certain one of us has done this at some stage in our lives...

D: Yeah, the problem is you can never remember any of it.

I dare ya to put one or two packs of Mentos in your mouth, then drink two litres of Diet Coke...
Paul, Dublin

D: Whatever you do, don't try this at home. Try it in someone else's home so you don't have to clean up the mess.

Put a tablespoon of baking soda in your mouth and then squirt in a mouthful of vinegar. Shut your mouth and keep it shut until the fizzing stops. This will most likely be quite unpleasant, uncomfortable and will result in excessive foaming from mouth and/or nose – but it won't kill you.
Cillian B

Drink a glass of water from the Liffey.
Ciaran

We dare ya to go into a café that has free refills and try to get as many refills as possible without being asked to pay again. But here's the catch: you have to walk in with buckets so you can keep emptying your drinks into them.
Aisling & Ailbhe, Dublin

I dare ya to drink 250ml of wee wee.
Hamza, Dublin

D: Phew! Thank goodness Hamza only wants us to drink 250ml. Any more and we'd puke.

Set up an off-license outside an off-license and sell the booze at a very low price.
Shane, Castlebar, Mayo

I dare ya to go into a pub and buy a few drinks and then start to auction them in the pub.
The lads from Aran

D: And...SOLD! To that bouncer guy waving his arms furiously.

I dare ya to drink a pint glass of sour milk.
Shane, Co Sligo

I dare ya to chug a pint of vinegar.
James

To go into an 'old man's pub' and put swizzle sticks, umbrellas and fancy straws in their pints, as well as pieces of exotic fruit on the side. See how long you can get away with it without them knowing who's doing it.
Suzanne, Dublin

OPERATION PINT-STEAL

I dare ya to sit at the bar in a pub. As someone orders a pint and is paying for it, pick up the pint and drink it. Then thank them for the pint and leave.
Jill, Dublin

A: Sometimes we get dares that we aren't excited about carrying out and this was definitely one of them. I mean, come on, we've all seen how aggro people get when someone even spills a little drop of their drink so we couldn't even begin to imagine what would happen when we drank their whole drink and walked off!

The dare says to do it inside a pub but because of the classic pub ambiance, it's too dark to film so we had to pounce on the outside pub drinkers. Plus three cameramen sitting on stools on the other side of the pub might have given it away.

We picked the first few 'victims' ourselves while the crew hid close by filming. Reactions ranged from one woman thinking I was a homeless person of some sort (thanks very much for that!) to two other lads saying they didn't want to be broadcast because they were having sneaky pints during work hours. Eventually though the producer and director felt we were cherry picking our targets a little and decided to scout for possible targets ahead of us.

Now let me tell you one thing about TV producers. They don't care about what danger the people they are working with are put in and what situations they help embroil them in as long as it makes good TV. So that's why the first mobile phone call we got was something along the lines of this:

Producer: "Right lads, go up to the group of three blokes outside the red brick pub around the corner."

Andrew + Damian: "Cool, no worries, which lads are they?"

Producer: "Don't worry, you'll know them. But be careful you pick the right group 'cos there are a group of lads beside them who just look plain dangerous!"

Line goes dead.

FUN!

Right! So our objective is to take the drinks belonging to the three blokes who look less likely to beat our heads into the table. We could see them while we were peering around the corner. Mid-twenties, jeans and black t-shirts and seemed to be enjoying themselves. Let's see what happens when their drinks are removed from the equation.

The good thing with stealing pints from a group is while you're knocking it back, the pint owners are looking at their friends to see if they know you, assuming you're a pal of theirs pulling your old 'knock back a pint entrance'. By the time you've finished it, they've realised that no one there knows you and you're just a measly drink thief. However, these three blokes were more clued in than that.

Trying to block out the sensible part of our brains which told us not to, we weaved through chairs and tables to get to our 'three blokes' target. One table of three was covered by a lot of ripped denim, tattoos and one eye patch so we assumed that was the 'plain dangerous' group.

We swooped in and grabbed a pint each, both nearly full. The pint owner I went for reacted like a hawk and clawed his pint back almost immediately. Damo managed to down a bit of his pint as its owner was pulling at his arm to get it back. Now for 'Operation Get the Heck Outta There!' We got away from them and their denim pirate neighbours just in time.

So it was people like those groups that made us not massively surprised when we eventually got a glass thrown at us by a girl because we took her friend's drink. I mean that is a bit of an overreaction; she wasn't even Irish! We think it was because we decided to take her friend's drink and not hers and as a result she got slightly offended. When I say slightly I mean majorly and when I say offended I mean violent. She seemed like the perfect match for another bloke who asked Damo if he wanted some more of his pint by trying to pour it over his head. He somehow didn't get the irony of being annoyed at someone taking some of his drink but then not minding losing the rest of it.

Of course we went back to all the pint-less victims

and shouted them all a round of drinks. Each time the people went from being furious to 'ah sure take a seat ya thievin' b*stards' and we all had a drink and a laugh.

So there you go, a sure fire way of getting people to hate you in an instant while strolling around town on a summer's day... but a cheap way to get hammered.

RESTAURANT

Set off stink bombs and fart spray in a packed restaurant and ask people if they farted.
Derrick, Allenwood

Go wine tasting with a group of five people. When the tasting is done, drink ALL the spat-out wine from the spittoon.
Nichola & Luke

I dare ya to have a game of 'bollox' in a posh restaurant.
Owen, Drogheda

D: Be careful, some restaurants might just bring you the pig's bollox on the menu.

I dare ya to go into a McDonalds and order a super meal. Every time the staff member gives you an item, throw it in the bin. When they add it all up say: "I didn't get anything."
Lee

Walk up to a fancy restaurant and stand outside the window. Sneeze all over the window and then try to wipe it off!
Darren, Dunboyne

Dress as two butchers with white hats, blood-stained overalls, boots, etc. Deliver a slab of meat/cow to a veggie restaurant with an invoice...insist the invoice is correct.
Mr Riley, Knock

I dare ya to go into a really posh restaurant and order the most expensive meal. Then pay with your shoes and in a knacker accent say: "I forgot me wallet."
Ruth, Co Dublin

Go into a really posh restaurant and when all is quiet, let off the hugest, loudest, smelliest fart ever in front of the waiter!!
Tara, Enniscorthy

I dare ya to go into a restaurant and start eating off other people's plates, telling them that you are a food inspector!!
Chris, Ballymun

Pretend to be health inspectors and close down a popular restaurant.
Caroline, Co Kerry

I dare ya to go into a restaurant and order a meal. Say you don't like it and throw it in the waiter's face. Then get people to leave the restaurant and start a protest against it outside.
Eoin, Kilkenny

Go to a fancy restaurant, sit down and get ready for dinner. When the waiter comes for your drinks order, ask for a bottle of "1995 Screaming Eagle Cabernet Sauvignon" – it's only €4,000 a bottle! When the waiter comes back and pours you a taste, tell him you don't like it and that you want something different – a bottle of house red at €22.50 a bottle. Watch the management freak out! It's not illegal in any way!

Cathal

I dare ya to go into a restaurant with a bib and spoon and get people to spoon-feed you.

Ricky, Cobh

Take your girlfriend to a fancy restaurant; your girlfriend being an inflatable one with that surprised look on her face. Pull her chair out for her, order her favourite wine, a meal and then pop the question during dessert. If she says no, pop her.

Daniel & Tammie, Perth, Australia

I dare ya to go to a fancy restaurant and eat with your hands only. You have to order soup.

Joe, Dublin

I dare ya to go into a café or restaurant and take a bite of somebody's food.

Keith, Co Tipperary & Kate

D: Great way to get fed for free. We did this one with some alfresco cafés off Grafton Street. Andrew and our mate Darren pointed out a very attractive brunette woman who was eating a bagel.

I went up to her, interrupted the conversation with

her and her friends, took the other half of the bagel and ate it. It turns out the targeted woman was Caroline Morahan, TV presenter and journalist. That's why Darren and Andrew pushed me in her direction. Caroline didn't mind at all and even let me have more off her plate. We had a conversation and as far as she knew, I was some Aussie scab stealing food. She's not 'Off the Rails' at all!

BE CRAZY

Shower in milk and wash your hair with jam.
Dee, Edinburgh

I dare ya to throw lots of pies at people, oh yeah!
Joe, Dublin

Go around for a day with porridge in your shoes.
Katie, Dublin

Get one of the lads to constantly pie the other one as he goes about his day. The one getting pied isn't allowed get angry and has to ignore the other one's presence.
Randy, Ballsbridge

I dare one of the boys to get his whole body lightly sprayed with water, then covered in salt, and then roll himself over a blanket of crushed ice on the ground. Stay still for a couple of minutes after.
Simon

D: It's just a guess, but I think Simon's a barman.

FAST FOOD

Stand outside a pizzeria. When someone comes out with a pizza box, slap it out of their hand and act as if nothing happened.
Paul, Cork

I dare ya to cause a riot at the McDonalds on O'Connell Street.
Kenneth, Kerry

I dare ya to get one of those Fisher Price cars that toddlers have and go through a car wash in it. Then, to show off your shiny car, drive through a McDonalds drive thru.
Aisling, Tralee

Set yourselves up as bouncers on McD's in The Square, Tallaght. Refuse entry to anyone in a tracksuit!
Dee, Gorey

Pretend that you work in a chipper and drive around Drimnagh asking people do they want chips. You have to get a cooker in your car and cook the chips.
Darren, Dublin

I dare you two crazy cats to go into Burger King dressed as Ronald McDonald, buy a meal and sit down and eat it.
Paulie, Ballyfermot & Gary, Kildare

Go into McDonalds during lunchtime dressed in tuxedos. Set up a table and demand table service.
Terri

A: We carried this dare out while we were at the Edinburgh Comedy Festival in 2006. Let me tell you we were very excited about it because this is something that both of us wanted to try out at some stage in our lives!

So we popped on the glad rags and headed for McDonalds on Princes Street, Edinburgh with some fancy cutlery and kitchenware.
As we walked in we realised it was gonna be more

difficult than we thought as it was a BUSY day in good old Mickey D's. Undeterred we headed upstairs and set out our table with wine glasses, tablecloth, napkins, plates, side plates and very fine silver cutlery. After a few moments of no service we decided to take matters into our own hands, or fingers as it were, by clicking very loudly and yelling: "Garçon".

Finally we got some attention. We asked if we could see some menus and I don't want to generalise or anything but I have never seen someone look as confused as this young staff member did at that stage. Of course she had to go and get help and when she came back with the manager we knew we were going to be on the road to success. Damo turned on his Mr Smooth switch and sweet talked the lovely lady into taking our order and even pouring our thickshakes for us! SUCCESS! We did get a lot of looks from a) Some kids who looked like we were living their dream, b) Some tourists who thought this was the normal way to act and c) Everyone else.

So there ya go, if ya wanna get table service in McDonalds all you have to do is dress nicely and treat them with respect. Oh and apparently they thought we were a gay couple on our anniversary so that might help as well.

A NIGHT ON THE TOWN

PUB TO CLUB

Walk into a gay bar and ask: "Can I bum a fag?"
Padraic, Galway

I dare ye to go into a pub and go behind the bar and pull your own pints!
Stephen, Roscommon

I dare ya to go into a nightclub in just a thong and see how long it takes you to get chucked out!
Alan

A: Sure that's practically what people are wearing to nightclubs these days. It is the only place in the country that women feel depressed if they DON'T get felt up by random men all night.

I dare ye to dress up as horses and go into bars, getting up the noses of barmen as ye order nothing but salted peanuts.
Karen, Kerry

Stand beside the queue for a busy nightclub, or outside its toilets, holding up a sign "cocaine for sale".
Sarah, Carlow

See how many times you can get turned away from the same pub/club. When you get turned away, come back and keep trying to get in. Even if they want to let you in, you've gotta do or say something stupid to make them not let you in. After a while get creative; try sneaking in, dressing up – that sort of stuff!!

Eamonn, Swords

Go to a bar and approach a few girls. After you've been talking for a while ask them to join your cult, because they are 'the chosen ones.'

Brian, Meath

Go up to a girl in a pub (she must have friends beside her) and say: "Hi, you're not really my type but it's gettin' late in the night and I'm not fussy so do you fancy coming back to mine?"

Claire, Dublin

Get a mannequin and dress it up and pretend that it's a mate that's hammered. Pretend you're holding him up while walking down some road. Then let him slip in front of a passing car.

Daire, Letterkenny

I dare ya to sleep in some random guy's front lawn and see what he says in the morning!

Sean, Arklow, Co Wicklow

D: Ha! We've all done that at some point...haven't we?

I dare ya to go into a nightclub and to use the following chat up line on as many women as possible: "Buy me another drink, you're still ugly."

Jack, Kilkenny

Go up to someone (either a guy or girl) as they are trying to light a cigarette and every time they use their lighter, blow it out before they get a chance to light the cigarette!
Claire, Galway

Go up to anyone smoking and ask for a cigarette. If you get one, crush it in front of their face and say thanks.
Timmy, Dublin

I dare ya to milk a couple of goats on Temple Bar Square on a Friday during the happy hour.
Estelle, Liverpool

D: Happy Hour for the goats it sounds like...

Go into a pub and drink out of the tap.
Anto, Wicklow

I dare ya to go to a club with electric guitars and rock instruments and climb on top of a table and perform a song. Then act all rock and roll and smash a guitar!
Sinead, Carrick on Shannon

Go into a bar and ask for four or five drinks. Say you are going to the toilet but leave the bar instead.
Seamus, Co Limerick

Walk into a pub, chat up a woman, order her the most expensive drink in the house and let her pay for it. Then walk straight out.
James, Mayo

Try to get into three posh night clubs in the one night dressed as a woodland animal.
Eamonn, Smithfield

I dare ya to pretend to be Siamese twins with your crotch attached to his ass.
Barry, Co Limerick

I dare ya to dress up as Native American warriors (feathered headdresses, war paint, bows and arrows, etc.) and prowl Temple Bar for a hen party who are wearing those tacky pink cowboy hats. (This should take about five minutes on any Saturday night.) When you find one, you have to launch an 'attack'. Encircle them, while whooping war cries, hold them at arrow point, and escort them to the Molly Malone statue, insisting that they make an offering to the statue which you revere as a deity.
Abie, Dublin

AT THE FLICKS

Go see a film and repeat every word the main character says loudly. When security try to kick you out, play a game of hide and seek with them.
Robbie, Celbridge

What ye should do is go into your nearest cinema dressed as a pair of horny parrots and fly up to the front row. Make sweet parrot love for everyone in the cinema to see, shouting things like: "Squawk, who's a pretty boy then?" and "Oh yeah you like that you dirty parrot b***ard".
Jamie, Ennis, Co Clare

Go to see a film in the cinema that you've already seen. Stand up and start telling everyone what's going to happen.
Sharp, Co Meath

A: This could also be worded as: "Go to the cinema and be a dickhead for the whole film".

Go to the cinema dressed as a pirate with a poorly hidden camcorder in your hat.
Stephen, Dublin

Act like Father Ted and Dougal and protest outside a cinema – 'down with this sort of thing'.
Patrick, Sligo

Go to a cinema and see how many films you can get kicked out of by only using techniques such as popcorn throwing, kicking the backs of seats, letting your mobile phone ring, talking loudly during the movie, changing seats four or five times during the film...
Conor, Co Dublin

Put glasses on a sheep and take him to the cinema in a buggy to see a film.
Denise & Ashling

D: "One adult and one 'child' please."

Get a very large, but real-looking, afro wig and go to the cinema and sit in front of the biggest guy you see.
Finbarr

Dress up in some 80s *Fame*-type outfits and go into the cinema during a busy viewing of some film. (You can pick.) Sit and watch the film like everyone else until 27 minutes into the film. Then get up and go to the area in front of the screen. Do interpretive dance until you get stopped by security.
Elaine

A: I like how detailed this dare is - especially the fact that we have to do it at 27 minutes into the film. Also thank you Elaine for letting us pick the film.

This might lead to GBH. From Monday, both lads spend the whole week getting as many dates as possible for a film on Friday night. Bring name tags for your dates so you remember who's who. The winner is the one who has the most dates.
Pierce, Armagh

D: And now we get a bit classier...

Go to some classical opera gig somewhere, start moshing and try to get everyone else to start a mosh pit.
Adelaide, Cork & John, Kilkenny

WHAT HAS BALLS AND SCREWS OLD LADIES...

I dare yous to go into a packed bingo hall and keep shouting "Check!" every time you get a number on a bingo card.
Edel, Balbriggan

Sit in the back row of *The Late Late Show* audience and hand out letters to people in that row that spells 'Pat is a Plank'. Then all of you hop up together and hold up the letters .

Keith, Smithfield

D: Good ol' Pat. We wanted to get our pointer stick onto *The Late Late* for an interview. Then a Stick can talk with a Plank.
(...Oh we meant bingo screws old ladies, not Pat Kenny.)

GAY NAZIS

Dress up as Nazis and go chat up men in a gay bar.

Anna, Dublin

A: Late on a Saturday night you may find people going into gay bars dressed as whatever they like but I don't think you really see people dressing up as Nazis very often.

We had to do this after one of our live shows in Edinburgh. So we popped along to a very busy gay bar in the middle of Edinburgh on a Saturday night in our full military wear. People had warned us we wouldn't get in on a Saturday night; "it will be really busy", "you aren't even gay", "it will be regulars only" and, oh yeah, "you are dressed as Nazis." I guess we must have looked very gay because we walked straight in, no problems at all.

We went straight up to the bar and bought a round of the gayest drinks we could think of – Watermelon Bacardi Breezers all round. We stationed ourselves at a table and it wasn't long before we were chatting away to a few lads. We had a bit of a boogie and, to be honest, a great time. Before we knew it we had to head off. We walked in expecting to be killed but then when we were leaving all we could hear was:

"Hey everyone the Nazis are leaving!!! Hugs and photos for the Nazis!!!"

Classic.

ON THE STREETS

Lick the face of everyone you meet. Then say: "That's tasty!"
Killian, Sligo & Christina, Galway

Walk up to total strangers who are having a conversation. Interrupt by saying: "Excuse me, I'm nosy. What's going on?" Bonus points if you do it with someone that got pulled over by a policeman.
Ciaran, Cavan

I dare each of you to give a full-on proper wedgie to ten people you see with visible underwear, eg girls with their thongs showing, jocks half way up lad's backs etc.
Orla, Roscommon

Go around Dublin shouting: "I have no willy coz mammy said it was dangerous"!!
Class 351

Walk around Dublin with an 'I love Boggers' t-shirt.
Paddy, Kildare

Sell armpit hair to people in Dublin at €20 a batch.
Sean, Swords, Co Dublin

A: This makes me wonder how much armpit hair good old Seany has under there...hmmm...

D: Put me down for €60 worth.

I dare ya to go around Dublin and see who is the first to get ten men to let you shave some hair off their chest – the loser has to wear the hair as a beard.
Chloe, Galway

Run down O'Connell Street wackin' each other with big branches.
Andrew

To ask a random person on the street if you can have back the condom you lent them last week.
James

I dare ya to offer to shine people's shoes and spit on them.
Michael

D: Spit on the shoes or the people? Either/or I suppose...

I dare ya to pretend to be French and ask strangers where the nearest gay bakery is.
Michael, Dublin

I dare ya to bring back the S in Stringfellows! Strip for passersby. Who knows? You guys might be able to re-open it with your talent!
Damien, Dublin

I dare ya to go around Dublin talking to strangers, finishing every sentence with the words 'without my pants'. Your trip should include a visit to an Ann Summers shop, Knobs and Knockers on Nassau Street and an Easons bookstore.
Laragh & Cathy, Greystones

D: Easons?!

Dress up as a pair of 'emo' kids and hang out at Central Bank on a Saturday and try to make as many metal head/goth friends as possible.
Jade & Michelle, Drimnagh

Go around Dublin city and pick out random people who are smoking. Grab the cigarettes off them and stamp them out on the ground while quoting anti-smoking slogans. Make sure you're smoking yourself at the time!!
Coll, Dublin

Disguise yourself as a postbox. Then when people place post in the slot, run away with it and throw it down the drain.
Horatio

I dare ya to go up to people and try and buy random things off them, maybe their trousers, a watch or a hat.
Rhys & Nathan, Co Wickow

Go around town and ask random people in a Dublin accent to "Fight them for their shoes".
Conor & Matthew, Dublin

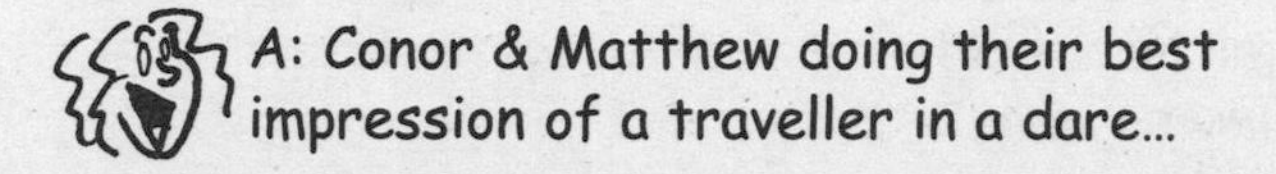
A: Conor & Matthew doing their best impression of a traveller in a dare...

I dare ya to walk around in bubble-wrap suits jumping at people screaming "pop me, pop me" and then run away screaming like a freak!
James, Galway

Start conversations with random people only using the sentence: "Can I stroke it?"
Kilian, Santry

To sneak up behind someone reading on a bench and begin quietly reading their book.
James

D: And if it's a 'Where's Wally?' book, point out where Wally is.

A: I like the idea that in Damo's head people go to a bench to read a 'Where's Wally?' book.

Follow people around spraying everything they touch with Dettol.
Ellen & Karen

Stand beside someone and start scratching your crotch. Say: "These crabs are very itchy."
Simo, Westmeath

I dare ya to see if you can hug ten drunks on the streets of Dublin. Hey you never know, you may find your soul mate.
Shane, Derry City

Set up a stall face painting children. Make a mess of all the children's faces. Make them cry and refuse to draw girly things for girls and boy things for boys. Tell their parents that now you've begun painting you will have to finish it.
Edith

HEY GOOD LOOKIN'

Go up to girls on the street and tell them you were dared to ask the ugliest girl you could find to go out with you. They will be thrilled to find out that they are that lucky girl!!
Roughmog, Co Kerry

Go up to a hot chick and ask for her mum's phone number.
Gavin , Kilmacud

Walk up to a kissing couple and start shouting: "What are you doing with my girlfriend?"
John, Co Meath

Go up to a couple and ask the man (when the girl is listening) does he remember you from a gay bar.
Ian, Cobh

I dare ye to dress up like nerds and try and get five fit girls' phone numbers in 30 minutes; that's five girls' numbers each, hee hee.
Marie, Roscommon

A: I want to take this opportunity to thank Marie for assuming we could get five fit girls' numbers without being dressed like nerds. I think this would be the most difficult dare of all.

I dare ya to go up to a woman and start poking her hair. Ask her where did she get the wig and compliment her on it!!
Laura, Galway

I dare ya to go up to five people and ask them can you do their hair.
Claire, Wexford

I dare ya to walk up and down Henry Street in a thong, wheeling a lawnmower, shouting: "Who wants their bush cut?"
Macker, Ballymun

I dare ya to go to a street and try and pick up girls with sh*t pick-up lines like: "I lost my number, can I have yours?" Only girls aged 18-22.
Chris, Dundalk

D: Good thinking. Girls any older than 22 would hit you a lot harder.

I dare ya to go to Ennis, Co Clare and get five or more women each to let you give them a foot rub.
Jade & Nicole, Co Clare

I dare ya to walk around Wexford and ask 20 people in half an hour if they prefer hard, semi-hard or soft cheese...
Rebecca, Wexford

D: You could also ask if they like 'blue vein' cheese.

Walk through Dublin with a tight pink boob tube and a micro mini skirt with a thong. Walk up to groups of people and start talking to them. Get closer and closer and start patting their heads saying: "Aren't you a good little thing?" And ask them to go for a walk with you alone!!
Kate, Co Kerry

Borrow some randomer's phone and call a chat line.
Eoin, Galway

I dare ya to see how many male members of the public will lie to your girlfriend on your mobile phone about where you were the night before...
John

BOOBALICIOUS

I dare ya to go up to any woman and feel her breast.
Kevin, Galway

D: If only it was that easy Kevin...if only...

I dare ya to walk up to any woman you see with large breasts and ask her: "Do you have a license for those?"
Rachel, Wexford

Go up to random women in the street and ask them where they got their implants done and how much did they cost. Ask if you can squeeze them to see if they feel real.
Brendan, Longford

I dare ya to walk around Limerick asking young mothers, of the 18-21 age bracket, why they didn't use condoms! And call them pram ladies!
Frankie, Limerick

I dare ya to go up to a woman, who's heavily pregnant or has a small baby with her, with a cup and ask if you can have some milk out of her breast because your tea's too hot...

Kate, Balbriggan

SEXUAL HEALING

Wander through the city wearing just a trench coat. Then randomly go up to women, open the jacket and say: "twenty euro, how about it?"

Jonny, Castleblayney

Go up to random young people on the street and talk about the sexual changes in their lives!! Tell them about the changes that you went through when you were that age!!

Cathal, Mayo

I dare ya to sit down beside someone in a public area and start reading a porno magazine. Then start asking the person beside you what they think of the people in the magazine.

Brino, Athlone

I dare ya to follow one person each and keep on asking them questions about their sex life.

Francis, Co Clare

I dare ya to go up to random people and ask them for some oral favours!!

Michael, Ardee, Co Louth

GOLDEN OLDIES

Find the oldest person you can and give them a nice big kiss... Of course it must include tongues!
Chris, Cork

I dare both of ye to go up to five women each who are aged over 50 and ask them what the following terms mean: reverse cowgirl, doggy style, 69, spanking the monkey, humping, poonami, boobies, deep throat, bumming, love juice and titty wank – the terms do not have to be explained to the women! Good luck!
Laoise, Galway

Go up and down Moore Street asking grannies do they want to feature in a gay porn film. Give them the option of either dressing up as a man or doing just a regular porn film. Say that they turn you on at that minute.
Sam, Dublin

STALK-HER

I dare ya to follow some randomer around for a whole day!
Ellen, Cork

D: Stalking can be tough, especially if your vict... sorry, randomer is active. We attempted this one and boy did it feel sinister...though it must've been a lot worse for our stalkee.

We went into a girly clothes shop to find someone to stalk. We picked a brunette with a red top (easy to spot in a crowd — we didn't find any women wearing high visibility fluro vests).

Why a woman you may ask? The dare does say 'randomer' which could be anyone but hey, its way creepier following a girl around. Plus there's a real element of risk. If a woman cops on that you're following her and calls law enforcements, you'd be locked up and more than likely have a restraining order taken out against you. If you're a bloke and you get caught following another bloke, the police will go: "Hey, stop following Jim, he doesn't like it." And that'd be it.

So our target, let's name her 'Meredith', spent a bit of time looking at and trying on clothes. Meredith's about mid-20s, 5'5 and got the 'girl next door' attractiveness going on. Only two pints until she's 'gorgeous' and that's quite good on the pint scale. She darted out and into another shop and spent a bit more time looking at and trying on clothes. We kept back a bit so as not to arouse suspicion but felt pretty dirty lurking around.

A: But to make it worse, as Damo was following 'Meredith', I was following Damo with the video camera and Zak and Darren (camera 2 and backup) were following me! I was a stalker's stalker.

D: Yeah so there was a chain of sleazy guys trekking after this one poor unsuspecting girl. She left the second shop and went onto the streets. We stayed right behind her, out of her eyeline and followed her into another shop. Then more time looking at and trying on clothes. Crap!

She still hadn't bought anything. This went on for three and a half hours! Just in different clothes shops!! Unfolding items, inspecting them, then putting them down. We were losing our minds! You think its awkward waiting outside the fitting rooms when your girlfriend is trying on a garment in a girly shop, try waiting outside the fitting rooms for the girl you're stalking! Especially when you're reading a newspaper with eye holes cut in it.

This went on for two more hours. She did buy something in the end; a blue top, lip gloss and a scarf, quite good taste. The four of us were bored to bits and hanging on by a thread. Then came some real action! A bus stop! As she stood waiting for the bus we were thinking we either come clean now or follow her on to the bus and go on a journey to God knows where.

I decided to go up and just start talking to her. 'What time's the bus?' kinda thing. As soon as she saw me approaching, she turned and started to walk away. I think she was weirded out and had seen us following her – I had suspected as much since I knocked that bin over back in Top Shop.

I thought I'd better follow Meredith to tell her we're not really stalkers and it was a dare. She whipped her head around and started walking faster away from me.

So I started walking faster too. She started power walking and so did I until I was running after her down the busy street.

As I ran I reached into my jeans pocket to pull out a flyer of the I Dare Ya live show with our photos on it. That way so she could see we weren't real stalkers; it was just a cruel and pointless prank. If only it was that easy.

I managed to get in front of her after she zipped around a corner. Panting, I lightly touched her shoulder.

"Excuse me, miss," I said to her horrified face.

As I said that, the flyer wouldn't come out of my pocket and the more I tried to pull it out the more it looked like...well. Meredith turned away with haste.

"Wait!" I shouted.

The flyer came free and I caught up with her and tried again.

In between breaths I showed her the flyer and explained the reason why she might have seen us pursue her. It wasn't our idea, free tickets for her and mates to the show; all that jazz. All the while her expression didn't budge from looking frightened. Then she attempted to talk to me and it all became clear. She was Polish with not a word of English.

Ouch. Now we look even more like stalkers, but really stuttering, clumsy, bad ones. I hope Meredith doesn't learn the words 'restraining order'.

Maybe we should've stalked a bloke.

OUT AND ABOUT

I dare ya to go to Tullamore in swimsuits and carry buckets and spades and ask locals where the beach is.
Joey & Deborah, Lucan

I dare ya to charge people money to cross the Ha'penny Bridge just like the old times.
Alan, Lucan

I dare ya to put a dummy into a body bag and ask people to help you throw it into the canal. You could try it in an area of Dublin that ends in an odd number...
Des & Pete, Blackrock

I dare ya to come to Cavan but have it mixed up with Navan! Go around looking for Navan tourist hot-spots.
Cian, Cavan town

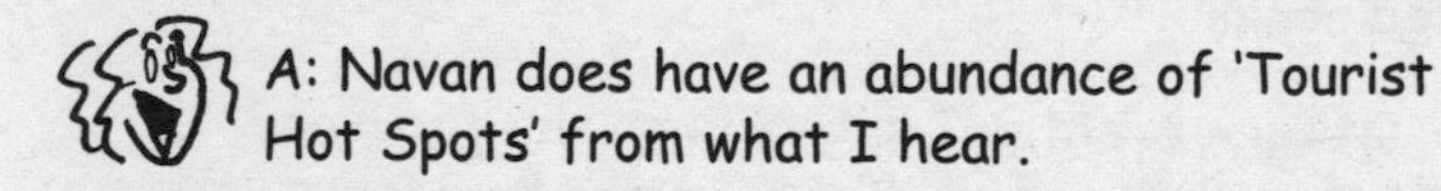

Visit Galway City and ask every girl with black hair and blue eyes will they marry you because they're your *Galway Girl*.
Siofra, Galway

I dare ya to have an 'I Love Kerry' parade in Cork.
Rach & Say, Co Cork

Walk around Limerick City dressed in drag, pushing a pram full of dogs.
Joe, Limerick

Chain yourselves to the Spire in protest to its creation.
Conor, Co Leitrim

Go to Ballyfermot and whisper into people's ears: "You faggot." See will you get away with that.
Niall, Dublin

Hand out flyers to every Southsider you can find informing them of the Government's plan to relocate residents from the Southside to newly formed Ballymun flats.
Stephen, Kildare

Go around Cork City with a water gun and start squirting people's private areas.
Dylan

I dare ya to evacuate St Stephen's Green due to adverse flooding.
Conor

Go to a County town bordering Dublin such as Bettystown. Change all the signs to Dublin and put up Dublin flags. Hand out leaflets welcoming the town to Dublin. Write out a list a specific ways to behave like a Dubliner. Advise people that there will be classes held to deal with the transition period.
Mark

I dare ya to go camping on Grafton Street. Get a gas cooker and roast marshmallows. Set up a tent and sing camp fire songs. See how long you last without a guard runnin' ya.
Sean, Galway & Jack, Kildare

D: Because Sean's from Galway we decided to give it a go in Eyre Square, in the centre of Galway town. Great fun. We pegged in our tent at sunset, had a gas cooker, roasted marshmallows and sang songs as dared. No one cared at all! Guards even walked past and gave us a nod. If anything, people wanted to join in. They would come up and ask for freshly singed mallows. Fun for the whole family!

Although location is important:

Camp out in South Hill for a night.
Rob, Limerick

D: Ah, South Hill, Limerick. I'll bring the marshmallows and the petrol, Rob you bring the safety goggles and bullet proof vests.

BUSKERS

I dare ya to track down a mime on Grafton Street and try to make him move.
Sean, Co Meath

Approach a male busking moving statue as a gay moving statue and try to woo them.
Ian, Dublin

Dress up like a mime (little black and white, French-style shirt required) and sit in a car that's parked in a handicapped parking space. Wait for someone to come and give you a ticket, then protest in mime.
Adam

I dare ya to go up to all the human 'statues' on Grafton Street and give them all a wet willy!
Sinead, Co Kildare

Go up to the human statues on Grafton Street with water in a bucket and a few sponges and start cleaning all their make-up off. After trying to wash them, ask for a tip for doing it.
Cillian

I dare ya to go to Grafton Street and spray silly string at the buskers!
Michael, Irishtown, Dublin

Go busking on Grafton Street. No musical instruments required... just bring a lighter and make sure you store up some noxious internal gases. Yes that's right – light your own farts for money!!
Daniel, Castleknock

Go busking outside a GAA match and when people throw money at you, throw it back at them and shout abuse.
Derrick, Allenwood

A: The problem with that dare is the assumption that we are good enough buskers to get money thrown at us...

I dare ya to take some money from a busker and walk away.
Antoin, Cork

Go onto the streets of Dublin and start a competition with the buskers, whether they know it or not, by standing next to them playing your own music louder.
Ali, Celbridge

Get some paper and draw some fake money! Then put it in a busker's hat or in a charity box!
Charlotte, Tipperary

I dare ya to go up to a busker, throw a €50 note into his hat and then say: "Shit, that was meant to be a fiver". Then as you go to change it, grab the hat and leg it, spilling the coins all over the place!
Emmett, Galway

CHARITY MUGGERS

I dare ya to get a job as a charity mugger and get fired within the first day by following people home on the bus and trying to get people to sign up to all the charities at once.
Mark, Dublin

I dare ya to go around town pretending to give people a survey on their personal lives and include the words: baps, crack and tits.
Laura, Dublin

I dare ya to go around Grafton Street in a wheelchair collecting for 'Pimp the Wheelchair' fund. When people give you money, get out of the wheelchair and hug them. I use a wheelchair and I think it would be hilarious.
Donal, Dublin

D: Hey if Donal says it's OK, then it's OK!

To stand in the middle of the street with one of those clipboards and ask people to sign your petition to have petitions and their canvassers banned. Keep them there for as long as possible bemoaning the fact that these people are wasting people's time.
Eric

FANCY A SNACK?

Offer cotton candy to civil servants.
Liam, Dublin

Walk around Cork City dressed as the Tellytubbies offering people custard. You must get ten people to eat the custard.
Roisin, Cork

Take a load of magic mushrooms and walk around the city! Great craic!!

Jeff, Dublin

CAN YOU TELL ME HOW TO GET, HOW TO GET TO...

D: We combined these two dares into one when we stopped in Castlebar, County Mayo:

I dare ye to go up to someone and ask for directions while taking your clothes off.
Gearoid, Mayo

Run up to a random person, give them the clothes you're wearing and run off.
Declan, Co Mayo

D: It was a drizzly day. Andrew staked out in the car with the video camera peeking out of the car window. I slowly paced the street looking lost, waiting for a passerby to ask for directions. First randomer walked up, a bloke in his 30s wearing a denim jacket, striding like he had somewhere important to be. His eyes were fixed forward as if the last thing he wanted to see was a skinny guy taking his clothes off.

"Excuse me mate, which way to the TF Royal?"

I interrupted his pace. He faced me and politely answered.

"Ah it's straight up this road on the right..."

As he's talking I took my jacket off and I hand it to him. He instinctively hinged his arm up and held it, then I undid my jeans and they fell around my ankles exposing hairy legs and knobbly knees.

"The heck with this," he said under his breath.

He dropped my jacket to the ground and continued striding down the road as if the faster he walked the easier it would be to deny what just happened.

Strike 1, no cigar.

Soon enough a guy and a girl wandered into view, early 20s, quite funkily dressed. Beanie hat, hoodies, shoulder bag, you get the idea. If 'funkily' isn't a word, it is now. Perfect target.

"Excuse me, where's the TF Royal?" (Same question got the first guy talking so go with what works.)

They both helpfully faced me, information filled their heads and the guy started.

"OK you go down here..."

I'm already disrobing; first my jacket, then shoes, socks. I dropped my trousers.

While this was happening the guy slowed his speech like a cassette player running out of battery power. Then they both just stood there in stunned silence. I then took my shirt off and handed it to the girl.

"Thanks," I said, then turned and ran down the road wearing only my Powdered Toast Man boxer shorts. As my bare feet slapped the wet ground I realised just how fast people can go from fully clothed to nude. It's quite a nice thought.

It's a hit! Run to home base!!

Meanwhile Andrew kept filming the two bewildered people laughing at what just happened. They watched me disappear over the hill and then glanced at each other realising I wasn't coming back. Well, I couldn't just run to the next street, spin around and walk back. I had to give the illusion I was running to the TF Royal. After all, I did ask where it was and I'd hate them to think I didn't hear any of their very helpful directions.

They were both still holding my jacket and shirt so they picked up my shoes, socks and jeans and placed them in the doorway of a pub. As the girl dropped my jacket down, she stopped, held out my shirt, inspected the front and back and checked the label before laying it in the doorway. Women just can't help themselves.

I returned to find all my clothes in a neat bundle in the doorway! Well if that's not a sign to call it a day I don't know what is.

WHAT THE WORLD NEEDS NOW

I dare ya to wrap somebody's car with wrapping paper and a big bow. When they return the two of you will sing 'happy birthday' wearing only thongs!
Elaine, Dublin

Walk up to random people and give them a BIG hug.
Aoife, Waterford

D: Ahhhh, that's lovely Aoife.

Stand in the street with loads of teddies and ask people to pick their favourite one. When they do, rip the head off the teddy and throw it at them.
Kevin, Stranorlar

D: Ah Kevin, you ruined the feel good vibe. But he's not done yet...

Walk up to someone with a hoody and pour some drink into it. Then put the hoody up over their head.
Kevin, Stranorlar

Find somebody who looks a bit unhappy and ask them to be your valentine. Buy them a bunch of flowers or something and make their day.
Aileen, Dublin

I dare ya to go up to someone you don't know and go over to them. Shake their hand and say: "I've found you, my long lost love. I've been waiting for this my whole life. Let's go home and celebrate."
Jennifer, Co Cork

Ask ten people for hugs and hold on for as long as possible.
Shane, Meath

SCRUBS

Pass yourself off as a doctor in a hospital for the day.
Andrew

Walk into the door of an optician.
Eoin, Galway

I dare ya to pretend that your hand is attacking you and try to get someone to call an ambulance.
Diarmaid, Youghal, Co Cork

Walk down Henry Street wearing a sign saying 'I worked in a sperm bank and got sacked for drinking on the job'.
Heffo, Ballymun

Walk out of hospital wearing a hospital gown with a portable drip and try and get into a taxi.
Paul, Dublin.

Dress up as a sperm, go to a maternity hospital and ask to see your child.
Davy

LIGHTS, COSTUMES... ACTION!!

I dare ya to go down Grafton Street wearing nothing but a sign saying 'Dubes and uggs are for twats!'
Gabrielle, Dublin 4

Dress up as a prostitute and walk around the streets of Dublin getting people to sponsor you!
Sonia, Co Offaly

Dress up as a mad scientist. Get an object and throw it at someone and shout: "This (name of object) will explode in 5 seconds, everybody run". Then run away!
Pugsy, Winter Wonderland

I dare ya to dress up in an Indian costume and do a rain dance on a wet day in Dublin!
Hugh, Blackrock & Shane, Sligo

I dare ya to dress up as Molly Malone and try and sell cockles and mussels to people.
Robert, Co Meath

Dress up as Vikings. Go to Collins Barracks and ask for "your" ship back.
Michael

I dare ya to dress up as Vikings and start chasing after the Viking Splash tour bus on horseback calling them posers.
Brendan, Dublin

Dress up as goths and sit outside the Central Bank weeping, while holding hands on a Saturday afternoon.
Rob

Dress as male prostitutes and stand outside the Dáil and proposition the TDs and ministers as they enter.
Mark, Dundalk

Dress up as a litter fairy and chase after people who drop litter.
Sinead, Dublin

I dare ya to set up as if you're painters beside the spire. Then pretend to paint the spire yellow!!
Mark, Wicklow

I dare ya to walk around dressed up like a goth saying: "Armageddon is coming" and handing out leaflets for a car wash.
Michael, Laois

Dress up as your favourite *Mortal Kombat* character and walk up to random people in the street and challenge them to *Mortal Kombat*!
John

A: I assume we wouldn't actually have to 'finish them!' like in the game, in other words actually ripping their spine out?

Put temporary metal fences, like the ones you see at building sites, around the spire and put up a sign saying: "Demolition of the spire will commence on xx/xx/xxxx" (Put in some date). Pretend to be trying to start a chainsaw that will not start.
Thomas, Westport & Garreth, Finglas

I dare ya to pretend to be making a music video in the middle of the street and ask people to join in and start dancing with you. (Don't take no for an answer.)
Hazel, Roscommon

I dare both of ye to dress up as female Irish dancers (full gear – wigs, shoes, knee high socks) and perform on Grafton Street.
Angela, Waterford

Alright lads, I dare yis to put on some leathers and imitate the famous music video by The Verve, 'Bittersweet Symphony'. Barge your way up the street (without seriously hurting anyone!) while singing the song.
Kev, Lucan & David, Cork

I dare ya to go to O'Connell Street or Temple Bar and do a full performance of the Rocky Horror Show, just the two of you. Each character must be included and full costumes worn!
Sarah B, Dublin

Dress up as Oompa Loompa's and sell chocolate apples on Moore Street.
Conor, Dublin

I dare ya to go downtown dressed head to toe as pirates. Proceed to break into song on park benches, attempt to pillage a vending machine and attack people with plastic swords.
Eva, Louth

I dare ya to dress up as Jack Sparrow and Will Turner from *Pirates of the Caribbean*. Then do the following: have a sword fight in a busy street and go on a treasure hunt in the Phoenix Park.

Aoife, Sligo

There's a guy in Wexford town who dresses up as Darth Vader and stands on the main street every day. He holds a sign for some shop. It would be the funniest thing ever if you get a couple of guys to dress up as Luke Skywalker and the rest of them *Star Wars* guys and attacked your man with them plastic light sabers.

Neil, Wexford

I dare ya to shove a brillo pad up your arse and see who can run the farthest!

Luke, Sligo

D: Good idea Luke, race ya!!

I dare ya to go out onto a busy street in leotards with a stereo and some work-out music. Start doing an aerobics session and try to get people to join in.

Shane, Killiney

I dare ya to unicycle down O' Connell Street as ninjas.

Grainne

To walk down O'Connell Street backwards, with a box on your head, and in shoes a size too small. This dare is only complete once you've made it from the top of Parnell Street to O'Connell Bridge. GO!

Craig, Dublin

D: You think that's random...

Walk around town with your underpants on your head, wearing a tissue stuffed bra and talk randomly to people around you. Then buy ice creams and throw them at people when they don't have a conversation with you.
Robyn, Dundrum

Go into Dublin Castle dressed in full armour and have a sword fight making use of all the different steps and levels (swords can be plastic or wooden).
The Debbler

Set up an archaeological dig outside the National Museum of Ireland while dressed as Indiana Jones.
Ken, Dublin

Tight-rope across the Liffey any way ye can, wearing fat suits.
J. Moses, Dublin

D: This next dare is an ace idea but spot where Jamie gets lazy towards the end...

Ye should set up what looks like a film set in the middle of the street. Grab passersby and tell them that one of the actors has gone missing and you need a replacement and fast. Tell them they will be in a big movie. Give them a two-line script and get them to learn it off and say it over and over again while a big sign that reads. "COMPLETE TWAT!" is lowered behind them. So as he/she is rambling out some random script onlookers are just walking past him/her reading the big sign behind him/her. The script that they have to read should be something like... I dunno, use your imaginations.
Jamie, Ennis, Co Clare

I dare ya to go around town in Dublin and ask strangers to help ye make a six-person pyramid on the street. There has to be three girls and three guys. Good luck!
Gearoid, Galway

Go around Dublin dressed up as the Devil and God. Pretend to curse boys and bless girls.
Eoin, Cork

Dress up as Aladdin with a "magic carpet" and ask people to give you a push.... as it just won't start!
Kate, Dublin

GAY PRIDE

Have a gay pride parade down main street Ballybofey.
Mark & Shaun, Ballybofey, Co Donegal

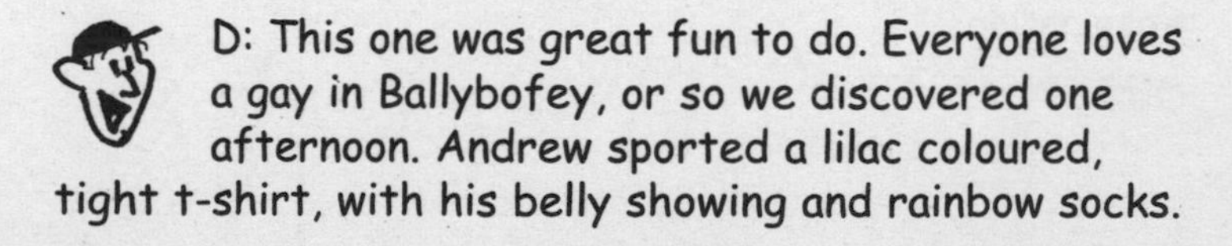

D: This one was great fun to do. Everyone loves a gay in Ballybofey, or so we discovered one afternoon. Andrew sported a lilac coloured, tight t-shirt, with his belly showing and rainbow socks.

I wore pink undies over my jeans and a white singlet with 'GAY AOK' written on in thick marker pen. We got a rainbow flag to wave and we were set to trot.

The dare says 'down main street Ballybofey'. It's a good thing they said that because there are no other streets in Ballybofey. Maybe Mark and Shaun just wanted to be sure.

We started at the bridge to Stranorla, the two of us linked arms and waved as we strutted through the town. We chanted: "We're here, we're queer, would you like to buy us a beer?" We got waves, honks, toots, even from the Gardaí!

When passersby noticed the video cameras they shouted: "Can I be on de tellie? Can I be on de tellie?" Adults are like: "This better not be on de tellie!" Where's the happy medium? I'll tell you where, mental people.

Strangers up for 'a bidda craic' joined us for a dance in the street and some photo opportunities outside Bonners pub, conveniently pronounced 'Boners'. Ah the fun.

That night we did a 'sold out' show in the Balor Theatre (had to drop the 'sold out' bit in, hear that Mum?) and unbeknownst to us Mark and Shaun were in the crowd. They seemed thrilled that we carried out their dare that day. We hope you boys are very happy together...

We received such a welcome response to our humble gay pride march that we're thinking of holding our own straight pride march there soon. We're going to wear badly fitting t-shirts with baggy jeans, kick a football along and chant stuff like: "We love boobs!" "Aren't women's bums great?" and "We're straight, it's great, only the doctor goes near our prostate!"

Ok, maybe we'll work on that.

POLICECOPS

CITIZENS ON PATROL

I dare ya to ask a Garda to move along.
Bobby, Rathfarnham

Take a policeman's hat and throw it into the Liffey. Then run off...
Niall, Ennis

Start a conversation with a female guard and then try to find out from her whether she's wearing a thong or just normal scundies.
Brian, Waterford

I dare ya to slap a Garda across the ass.
Colm

Go up to some mad lads in town and ask: "Where can I find the boss?" When they say: "What are ya talkin' about bud?" start shouting: "It's gonna go down, where is he?" Call for back-up on a radio. Say to them: "I'll spare you if you tell me where he is."
Ciaran, Lusk

I dare ya to dress up as a guard and arrest somebody on the street for walking too fast or too slow.
Cliona, Co Longford

I dare ya to dress as a police officer and try to arrest someone for an offence you made up.
Jason, Carlow & Amy, Ennis

D: What? Something like a 'can't think of an offence' offence?

Dress up as a Sheriff and his Deputy (badge, hat, boots, guns etc.) Go to Sheriff Street in Dublin and mingle with the locals – keep law and order! Duck and dive around the area. Stop cars. Question people. Spit. Take over Sheriff Street.
Mr Riley, Knock

Walk around pretending to be drunk until the cops come to arrest you. Then just be normal and act like you don't know what just happened!
Adam & Dara

I dare ya to follow a man or woman pretending that you are a special investigator hired by their other half on suspicion of them having an affair.
Miranda, Santry

Hire a private detective and have him follow you around but instead you follow him around.
Andy, Co Tipperary

I dare ya to let down the tyres of a Garda car, and then report it to them.
David, Cillian, Cathal & Eugene, Galway

I dare ya to pull a prank on the Gardaí – it would be very funny!!
Philip

D: Thanks for that Philip, any other ground breaking ideas?

I dare ya to set up a checkpoint outside a Garda station and try to stop a Garda car. Ask them if they have been drinking!
Barry, Cork

Ask a Garda if they want pleasuring.
Mary, Co Donegal

Wear a t-shirt saying 'F*ck the Pigs'.
Paddy, Kildare

D: You might be able to get away with this if you said it was a t-shirt about doing it with animals.

Handcuff a pedestrian to a railing or a locked bicycle.
Neil, Dundalk

Spend the day following a cycling Garda – preferably on a child's tricycle or dressed strangely. If questioned by the Garda, answer only in French or some other language. Never leave the Garda and see how long you last.
Ian, Dublin

I dare ya to get arrested for breaking into your own car.
John, Co Donegal

I dare ya to jump into a Garda car when it's stopped at traffic lights, and then say you thought it was a taxi!
Gary, Crumlin

I dare ya to dress up as an undercover Garda officer and flash your badge at people in cars. Demand they give you their cars for 'official police business'. See how many people give you their cars.
Kevin, Dublin

D: More fun than public transport.

Apparently it's illegal to piss in the streets. If you need a dump, however, a Garda is supposed to shield you from the sight of the public with his hat. Can you find out if this is true?

Donners, Co Kildare & Stuart, Wexford

D: I asked a Garda about this and he said: "Have you ever gone for a shit and wee hasn't come out?"

Good point.

So if you're going to try this, I'd say the guard would help shield your embarrassment and then fine you. But if the guard does shield you with their hat, you could throw it into the Liffey and run off!!

BANK JOB

Both of you walk into a bank, put on balaclavas and carry out transactions as normal...

Justine, South Dublin & Aoife, Leitrim

I dare ya to go into a bank and yell: "Everyone get on the floor." Count how many people get on the floor and then leave.
Gary, Dublin

Run into a post office with a toy gun and take someone hostage. Shout: "Give us the money or he/she gets it."
Adam

D: Then Robert here takes it slightly further...

I dare ya to rob a bank with guns or knives and shoot anyone who moves or breaths too loudly. Once you get the loot, run five blocks down the road and report yourself to the Gardaí.
Robert, Co Kildare

I dare one of you to spend the day in town conducting typical day to day tasks, while wearing a balaclava (eg shopping, buying stamps at the Post Office etc.)
Mel, Leitrim & Cian, Clonmel

I dare ya to get a taxi to a bank and tell the taxi driver to wait for you. Then a few minutes later, come running out of the bank with fake bags of cash in your hands and balaclavas on pretending to have robbed the bank. Tell the driver you'll kill him if he doesn't get away fast (use fake guns to do so).
Seanz, Limerick

D: I wonder how the driver would feel if you didn't tip him/her.

DOWN AT THE STATION

I dare ya to run into a Garda station naked.
Adam, Dublin

Call the guards and tell them you've caught chlamydia from a girl. Ask if there's any way you can press charges against her.
Amy, Ballymun

Go into a police station and start screaming "I DID IT".
Geena & Jack, Kerry

I dare ya to go into a cop station and tell them you have committed a crime. When they ask you what that crime was, tell them you downloaded 'High School Musical 2 – The Album' illegally.
Laura, Tallaght

I dare ya to go into a Garda station and start stealing stuff.
Jamie, Wexford

I dare ya to pretend to be blind and walk into a Garda station. Go up to the counter and ask them for two curry chips, one snack box and a leg of lamb. Throw them a twenty and say you'll be back, then walk out.
Emma, Clare

D: *Genius Emma, genius...*

GRAVE ROBBING DUO

Dress up as Burke and Hare and re-enact the mis-adventures of the grave robbing duo.
Tom, Edinburgh

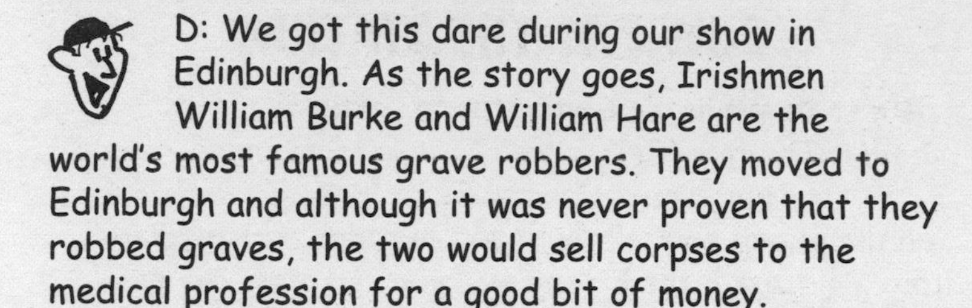

D: We got this dare during our show in Edinburgh. As the story goes, Irishmen William Burke and William Hare are the world's most famous grave robbers. They moved to Edinburgh and although it was never proven that they robbed graves, the two would sell corpses to the medical profession for a good bit of money.

When Burke and Hare wanted fresher bodies, they started killing people. They definitely murdered at least 16 people but some believe it was double that. They were caught when the missing bodies started appearing in front of medical students for dissection. Cool huh? Hare gave evidence against Burke in return for his freedom and William Burke was hanged in front of a huge crowd on 29th January, 1829. Funnily enough, his body was given to the medical profession to be dissected. Ha! Burke's skeleton is still kept in the Anatomy Museum at Edinburgh University Medical School.

So we never got around to doing this dare as we thought murdering people might be inappropriate. But as Burke was hanged and Hare got away, if we ever do re-enact their shenanigans, Andrew can be Burke.

ON ITS AXIS

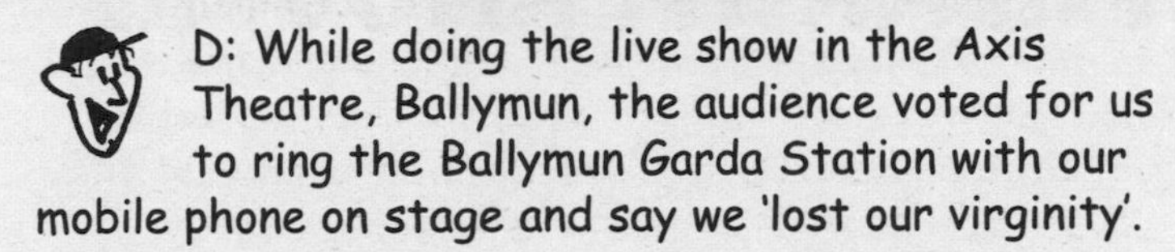

D: While doing the live show in the Axis Theatre, Ballymun, the audience voted for us to ring the Ballymun Garda Station with our mobile phone on stage and say we 'lost our virginity'.

We asked the crowd if they knew the number.

One woman immediately started rattling it off and as the audience members whipped their heads around she slowed the last few numbers, realising it might be a questionable ability to know it off by heart.

"At least I think it is," she finished off. Swish.

So we rang that number and what do you know, she was right.

Evidently as soon as the Garda on the other end of the phone heard the word 'virginity...'

'...Beep, Beep, Beep'

I HEAR YA KNOCKIN'

OFFICE

I dare ya to go into any office and start to put roll out grass down in the hallway.
Peter, North County Dublin

Pull a nik-nak on the Taoiseach's office in Drumcondra.
Colin, Donabate, Co Dublin

D: Or 'knock & run' - what 'nik-naks' are known as in Australia. How did we think that one up?

I dare ya to trick or treat (dressed as whatever you wish) around politician's offices, public offices etc. Only make sure it's not at Halloween and you can't leave without getting something!
Michelle, Sarah, Tom & Mick, Dublin

I dare ya to go into an office and refuse to let anyone answer their phones. Arm yourselves with only water balloons.
Barry

Play hide n' seek in the G.P.O.
Robbie, Celbridge

Pretend that you're a stripper and go into an office and start stripping.
Seamus, Co Limerick

Stand outside a building in Dublin and pretend that you are fumigating it. Tell passersby that they could get a harmful disease if they don't move quickly from the area and see who panics.
Aaron, Dublin

Go to an information office and take lots of leaflets. Divide them up into piles. Then take one from each pile and put them into a zip lock bag and try to sell them for €5.
Daniel, Galway

Eat old chewing gum off the underside of a desk.
Justine

I dare ya to get 40 women to walk into any office block and tell 40 men that they are the mothers of their babies.
Peter, North County Dublin

D: Pete does it again.

I dare ya to go into a lift in a busy office, set up a desk in it and when people try to get in, you ask: "Do you have an appointment?" Get them to sign a register and give them your phone number to ring up for an appointment for next week.
James, Greenhills & Claire, Dublin

I dare ya to arrive into the reception of my office and pretend to be a courier. Be naked and tell the receptionist that you have a rather large package for delivery.
Paul , Tallaght

A: Paul has come up with an amazing way to get yourself arrested very quickly. Either that or a dangerous way to chat up women. I can't see the results being that positive though...

HOTEL

I dare ya to walk into a hotel and don't bother speaking to reception. Just walk on in and jump into the pool.
Jake, Donegal

Call a hotel that allows pets and book a room at reception. Bring in your pets – a llama or donkey and some pet rabbits. Your family name for the register is Noah Doolittle!!
Paul , Swords, Dublin

I dare ya to go into one of the best hotels in Dublin dressed as Ghostbusters. Say there has been 'paranormal complaints' about this hotel. Say you need to 'inspect' it. Take out kitchen utensils and begin your 'inspection'. Refuse to leave until security comes.
Georgina

HOUSE CALL

I dare ya to see how many people's doors ye can knock on in one minute and then leg it.
Dylan, Sligo & Luke, Co Cork

I dare ya to go to a posh estate somewhere and have a game of 'nik-nak'. It's not as simple as ya think! Knock at the door and don't run! The longer you keep the muppet standing there the more points ye get!
Glen, Blanchardstown, Dublin 15

Knock on every door on O'Connell Street in half an hour!
Tony, Limerick

Shit in a bag and light it on fire outside someone's door and run away.
Adam G, Lucan

D: Old School. Nice.

I dare ya to call a locksmith pretending you have been locked out of 'your' house/flat. When he lets you in, pretend to rob the house and, to be a bit cheekier, ask him to hold the DVD player while you rob something else.
Leanne, Cork

I dare ya to be a door to door condom salesman. You must sell at least ten. Don't forget to describe your product through your own experiences.
Niall, Cashel

Lads, I dare ye to dress up and pretend to be TV license inspectors. Go round calling to houses asking them do they have their TV license.
Joe, Rathfarnham

D: The hunted becomes the hunter! Honestly do TV license inspectors know what 'free to air' TV means?

Call to random houses asking them to give you something for your 'Daz Doorstep Challenge'. You will then wash anything given to you on the doorstep using your own portable laundry device! You must wash at least 10 items.
John, Ballinamore

I dare ya to come to Finglas. Knock on every door and ask for money for charity.
Eddie, Finglas

D: The 'I'm going to need new underpants' charity.

Dress up as if it's Halloween and knock on doors. Keep insisting that it's Halloween. If they close the door on you, keep knocking. If they don't answer, egg them!!
Sinead & Peter, Draperstown

A: I like that Sinead & Peter have come up with an alternative solution just in case someone isn't at the house we call to. Egging is a lost art of abuse.

Knock on someone's door and say that you saw a book that said you are a lost relation of their family. But say that the book was in the library and the library got burned down...
Ciaran, Gorey, Wexford

I dare ya to go knock on a random house in Dublin and say: "I am your son, why did you put me up for adoption?"
Louise, Westmeath

Dress up as painters. Go to an estate and knock on people's doors. Have three tins of paint with you: red, blue and white. Tell them that a new English couple are moving into the estate and that you're going to paint their gate or fence in the colours of the English flag to make the couple feel welcome. Don't take no for an answer. Pretend to start painting by opening the tins of paint. Ask if you can put an English flag in the garden so the couple will feel extra welcome in Ireland. Tell them that you're going to paint all the fences in the estate the colours of the English flag. Tell them the good thing is that it's free of charge. I think it would be hilarious to watch people's reactions...
Paulie & Donal, Co Mayo

D: And sometimes the simplest ideas are often the best...

Go up to someone's door, knock on it and just stand there saying that they knocked on your door.
Alan , Sligo & Ronan, Dublin

Advertise as a clowning company. Visit your customer on their 'big day' as a drunken clown and just be generally intolerable and horrible at your job. Be sure to eat the guest's food and keep swigging from a bottle 'hidden' in a brown paper bag during your performance.
Adam

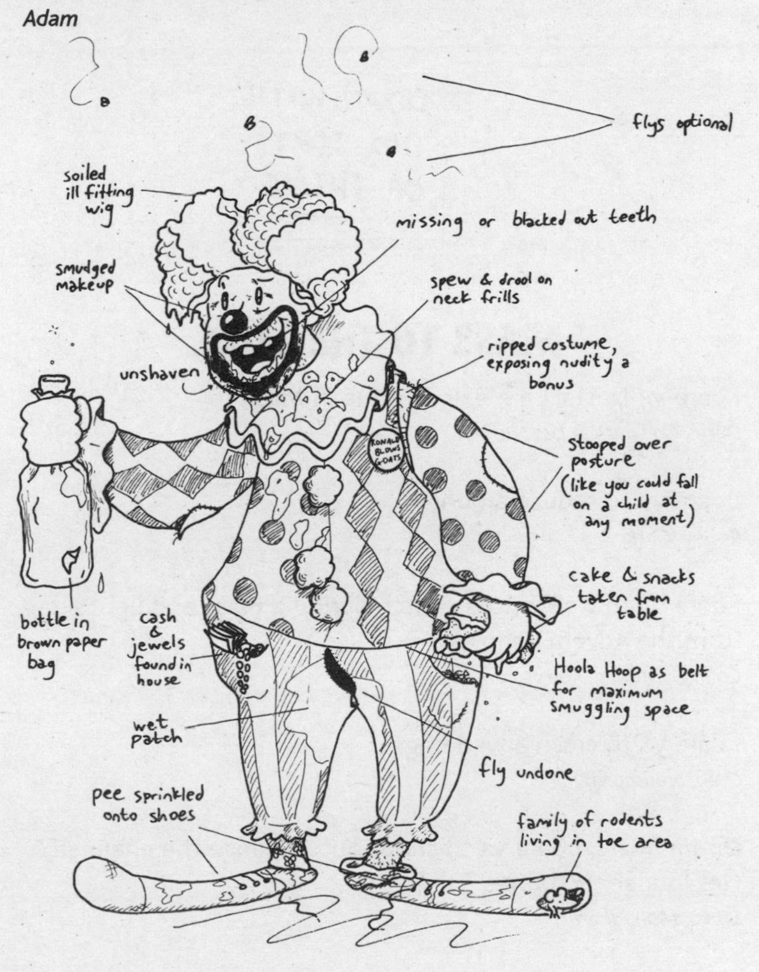

BAD RELIGION

MASS TO THE MAX

I dare ye to start a Mexican wave in Mass.
Daryl, Co Louth & Lisa, Dublin

I dare ya to seduce a nun!
Robby, Cork

I dare ya to walk into a church during a Mass and light a fag from the Advent candles.
Colin & Padraig, Kerry

I dare ya to crash a wedding.
Greg, Enniscorthy

During Mass, I dare ya to shout out: "Change the channel!" Get louder each time.
Stevo, Monaghan

Go to Mass dressed as Santa. Walk around the church giving people sweets.
Cathal, Galway

Go into a church during Mass and empty out the money from the baskets. Run through the church in a balaclava with the basket!
Colm, Co Cork

Go to a parochial house trying to sell communion flavoured condoms to the priest in charge.
Sean, Lurgan, Co Armagh

I dare ya to go to Mass and wait for the priest to say 'The Body of Christ'. Then start getting upset and say: "Ahh no, you're all cannibals!!" Then run out!!
Kieron, Wexford

Dress like a Nazi and go to Mass!
Mairead, Tuam, Co Galway

I dare ya to go into a church and exchange the statues and symbols there with those of another religion.
Colm, Galway

I dare ya to walk into Mass wearing a chicken suit and pretend you can't find a seat. Just walk around the front and eventually ask the priest can you sit in his chair.
Simon, Co Westmeath

I dare ya to preach about the Devil outside a Catholic Church.
Owen, Drogheda

Have an impromptu Mass in the main court area of Trinity College.
Sean

See who can swear loudest during Mass.
Philip, Derry

I dare ya to fake your own death for a week, attend your own funeral (disguised) and console your family.
Cillian, Mayo

A: That's probably one of the most extreme dares we have ever received. What a sick man you are Cillian...

D: ...but great for claiming life insurance.

I dare ya to go to a funeral home, one of ye get in the boot and the other one is to tell the undertaker that you have a body in the trunk of the car. Ask them what you should do with it.
Dylan Corcoran, Sligo

I dare ya to walk into Mass holding each others' asses and walk to the front so everyone can see you. When everyone's looking, pinch each others' asses and kiss each other. If you see anyone looking, ask them what they're looking at and just sit down like nothing happened.
Simon, Co Westmeath

Both of you dress up as priests. Have one of you sitting in his car outside a church (reading the Bible of course). Get the other to smash up the car, claiming the one in the car is possessed and needs to have an exorcism performed. Gather people off the street to drop to their knees around the car and say a decade of the rosary! Scream and shout that the Devil has got inside the other priest, but sure isn't he really in the car having a little nap and listening to his iPod!
Tracey, Co Kildare

Go into a church on Sunday and go up and start the Mass just before the priest does.
Mairead, Co Galway, Fintan, Rush & the Audience in Tripod, Dublin

A: This would be great to do as you could make up loads of crazy and ludicrous stuff and try to get everyone to believe you, then con them out of money and things like that... what?... That's already been done? Ooops!

I dare ya to go to Mass and when you are going up for communion, walk up with your pants around your ankles.
Mike, Co Cork

I dare ya to go into a church and when the congregation is singing, get your friend to ring you from outside. Tell everybody to stop singing so you can chat to your mate.
Fergal, Co Kerry

OUT OF THE CONVENT

Dress up as pregnant nuns and go to Christchurch in Dublin city.
Mark, Finglas

I dare ya to dress as nuns and walk down Grafton Street blessing people as they pass, holy water, the works, but especially the males if you know what I mean!
Sheila, Laois

Dress up as a priest and get really drunk in town somewhere...
Jon, Dublin

I dare ya to dress up as a priest and walk into a club looking for lap dancers.
Jamie, Limerick & Ciara, Co Galway

Drive through Knock with banners saying stuff like: 'GOD ISN'T REAL'.
James, Knock

I dare ya to walk into a chemist dressed as a priest and explain that you have an allergy to latex. Ask what condom they would recommend.
Eric, Co Cork

I dare ya to walk up to a priest and ask him if he's still supplying drugs to the kids in his parish!
Chris, Cork

Dress up as a Catholic priest (only one of ye at a time) and stroll around any busy street in Dublin city. See if you can chat up some women or men and ask them for some sex...
Franky, Limerick City

Kick a Bishop up the ass and get a picture of it...
Michael, Cork

Dress as priests and stand on a busy street preaching about God. Then, near the end, reveal subtly that you were talking about Morrissey. Show people your cross which actually has Morrissey written on it – 'Morrissey be with you!'
Dylan, Dublin

D: A Morrissey fan perchance Dylan?

Re-enact the Last Supper on O'Connell Street outside the Anne Summers store. Use blow-up dolls as the other ten disciples. Use French sticks, wine, water, M&Ms and dildos for your table display.
Mr Riley, Knock

I dare ya to dress up as a priest and tell people the Devil is coming and beware...
Sharon, Galway

D: Uuummm, that sounds like the usual priest practice.

BRANCHING OUT

Convert to five major world religions in five days: That's Christianity, Judaism, Hinduism, Buddhism and Islam.
Aran, Donegal

Dress up as a member of a new religious cult and recruit people to come to the new planet 'Damandrew' for free love 24/7. Do this dare straight after Sunday Mass at the chapel door.
Marty, Ballybofey

I dare ya to dress up in *Star Wars* Jedi uniforms and try to convert people over to Jedi. Tell them it's the new religion, see how many people tell you to p*** off!
Dave, Dublin

SCIENTOLOGY

Head into the Scientology HQ in Abbey Street and join up for a laugh. Tom Cruise t-shirts optional.
Keith, Smithfield

I dare ya to call Sylvester Stallone and try and convert him to Scientology.
Chris, Cork

CONFESS THIS

Dress up as a devil and go into a church for Mass!

Rory, Wexford

D: To dress up as the devil, you need:
Black tights (tracksuit bottoms will do)
Horns
Spiky tail
Plastic pitch fork
Goatee beard (drawn on will suffice)
A heck of a load of red body paint
Dark shoes you may have to run in

I dressed up as the evil one (seemed fitting as my name's 'Damian', son of the Devil according to *The Omen*) and with a Bible in one hand, pitch fork in the other, I strode past the towering Catholic wooden doors. This scared the 'bejaysus' out of a scarf wearing elderly lady who was on her way out of the church. She almost jumped out of her blue skin, then I calmed her by saying: "It's OK, it's OK. I'm just going to confession." She caught her breath, looked up at my red face and stated: "Well it's about time!"

Apart from that, there was a lot of staring but overall a positive response. They probably could see the repentance in Satan's eyes.

'TIS THE SEASON!

CHRISTMAS SHOPPING

I dare ya to go into a butchers looking for advice on how to 'bone your bird' (for Christmas dinner).
John, Cork

I dare you guys to do your Christmas shopping in Dundrum Shopping Centre wearing six inch high heels.
Maria, Dublin

I dare ya to go around Dublin after Christmas singing Christmas carols. You have to hound the shoppers to pay money to a makey-up charity!
Declan, Kill & Frank, Co Tyrone

Around Christmas time, run into a shop that has a tree and those fake wrapped-up boxes that look like presents. Like a hyperactive seven-year-old on Christmas morning, run over to them and rip open as many as you can!
Louise

A: That's just something everyone wants to do when they look at those boxes. I mean imagine the shops were just taking the piss out of us and they were actually all filled with amazing presents! The b***ards!

I dare one of you to dress up as Santa and walk around the shops casually. Then the other one of you, who would be dressed up as Mrs Santa, would run into the shop, pin Santa to the floor and start dry-humping him!

Mairtin, Co Galway

A: Sounds like someone caught Mammy kissing Santa one year and still has a few issues...

GROTTO

I dare ya to go into a shopping centre. Queue up for Santa and sit on his lap. Ask for a reindeer for Christmas. If the answer is no, look for an artificial reindeer say: "This will do". Then walk out with it.

Neasa, Co Waterford

Go to Santa's grotto in some supermarket and kick up a fuss. Give out to Santa because you didn't get what you wanted for Christmas last year.
Paddy, Newtown

I dare the two of you to dress up as Santa and an elf, the elf is to have a cap gun that looks real. As a child walks past, the elf shoots Santa and scares the child into thinking they're not getting presents because Santa is dead.
Rob, Tallaght

I dare ya boys to hold a Santa's grotto somewhere. One of you has to be Santa and the other an elf. Santa has to pretend to be drunk and scare the kids!! Don't forget to give crap presents!
Sean , Co Longford

I dare ye to go into Santa's workshop, sit on his knee and when he asks you: "What do you want for Christmas?" say that you want to go out with him! Give him a kiss on the cheek!
Rois & Steph, Clonmel & Jamie, Templemore

Dress up as an elf and go to a Santa's grotto. Try and be Santa's helper for as long as you can until you get caught!
Shane S, Dublin

Set up a drunken Santa's grotto on a city-centre street in Dublin – a la 'Bad Santa'.
Mel, Dublin & David

Go into Santa's grotto in one of the shopping centres in Dublin and do the normal stuff like sit on his lap, ask for something and then leave, except do all this in your boxers.
Jimmy, Lucan

I dare ya to go to Santa's grotto wearing a bondage outfit and sit on Santa's knee. Tell him what you want for Christmas!

Liz & Maria & Rois & Steph, Clonmel

D: Someone's been very naughty this year, haven't they?

HEY KID, ABOUT SANTA...

I dare ya to visit Santa and pull off his beard.

Colm, Kerry & Oran, Dublin

Go up to small children (make sure their parents are there) and tell them Santa, the Easter Bunny and the Tooth Fairy aren't real (also make sure they're small enough to believe in them).

Joe, Enniscorthy, James & Keith, Limerick

Pose as Santa in a toy shop and ask children to sit on your lap. Then suddenly burst out of Santa's clothes and tell them Santa ain't real!!
Paddy Heenan, Tipperary

A: What is wrong with all these people? Why would they make up lies about Santa not being real? That's just silly.

MIRACLE ON 34TH STREET

I dare ya to stick mistletoe on the wall or in the doorway of a shop, and ask a girl for directions while standing under it. After she (or maybe he) gives you them, look up, point to the mistletoe and try to kiss her/him!
Michael, Co Galway

I dare ya to walk down Grafton Street wearing a turkey costume holding up a sign saying: "Do not eat turkeys this Christmas. You are decreasing the amount of turkeys. If you do, our kind will take over Ireland and you will all be the Christmas dinner".
Brenda & Brendan, Drimnagh

Now that it's Christmas, be extra friendly and give hugs to business people. Target those who are in a rush.
Ruaidhri, Galway

I dare ya to dress up as Santa and Rudolf the Reindeer and stand on Grafton Street giving out leaflets on sex awareness and tell them to have safe sex over the Christmas season.
Brian, Ballyfermot & Brian, Dublin

D: This next dare is epic and one of my faves!

This is more of a 'concept' dare for the season that's in it. I'm not sure where the best place to do this is, but I reckon (as shall become clear) that either Bray Harbour, Blackrock Park or maybe St Stephen's Green would be the most amenable to a bevy of swans. So here goes...

First assemble the poultry. You will need one partridge, two pigeons or doves, three hens, four blackbirds, half a dozen geese and seven swans (swans being wild birds accounts for the location – as they would already be there in sufficient numbers). You'll also need a pear tree to put the partridge into.

Now to the guests. You need eight maids – now I won't insist on the virginal quality of the maids as this is located in Dublin and they might be difficult to find – so I figure get eight of the models that are always knocking around the newspapers and dress them up in maid uniforms. I'm no expert but I think you will need at least two dairy cows (four teats each) for them to be strictly 'a-milkin'.

Next, nine dancers. I think there's a ballet troupe from Russia hanging about at the NCH – although ordinary ballet dancers will do. Obviously we don't have Lords in this country, but on an equivalence basis senators will do. So you need David Norris, who seems to be always up for a laugh, and nine of his mates from the upper house. Drummers: Larry Mullen? Micka 'Don't F*ck With Me' Walsh? Dave Fanning probably knows a load of drummers. You need 11 of them with their drum kits.

Finally, 12 pipers should be available by mixing the Garda Band, the Army Band(s), the Artane Boys Band and whatever else you need – and plumbers won't do (they'd be more difficult to find anyway). Oh yes, you also need five 24ct gold rings.

Sorry I didn't send it to you sooner, I was on the piss. Merry Christmas.
David , Bray

D: Gold. And a Merry Christmas to you.

I dare ya to dress up as Santa and give out Christmas presents – with a twist! Give grannies anti-aging creams and tell them they will get young overnight, give nuns or priests toys for the bedroom and really annoy the people of Dublin!
David, Dublin

I dare Damo to dress up as Santa and Andrew to play the part of Santa's elf! It gets better... go into the middle of Temple Bar and start breakdancing. (Don't worry, you don't have to have skills for this, just go to the beat!). Then get a random person and get them to dance with you! Gowwan lads! Make us Balbrigganers proud!
Aimee, Balbriggan

I dare both of you to run down O'Connell Street wearing Santa thongs screaming: "Happy Christmas everyone!"
Sarah, Drogheda

I dare ya to go up to a house and act like Santa and give them toys.
Ryan, Tralee, Co Kerry

Walk into the Oireachtas dressed as Santa Claus in the middle of a meeting with Mary Harney.
Shaun, Donegal

Wearing only shorts, a Santa hat, leather driving gloves, swimming goggles, and footware of your choice, you must have a shower in the fountain in St Stephen's Green park.
The Horse, Balscadden

I dare ya to jet ski up the Liffey in a Santa Claus suit.
Vilius Vaiciulis, Crossmaglen

I dare ya to pretend to be the Irish Winter Olympic Curling team and go to the 7up Christmas on Ice at the RDS to practice.
Damian, Kildare

Get a tattoo of Santa on the back of your neck.
John, Tullow

I dare you guys to swim the Liffey in nothing but a Christmas thong!
Aoife

I dare ya to try out for a Christmas play for children!!
Grainne, Galway

D: What? Like a pantomime? I'd say after Christmas when we're all outta cash, that's exactly what we'll be doing.

Sit on top of the huge Christmas tree in the middle of Dublin city and throw hardboiled sweets at everyone who passes by!

Gill & Jonathan, Dublin

MERRY CHRISTMAS BALLYMUN

I dare ya to dress up as Santa and drive around in a car blasting Christmas songs from the stereo and shouting: "Ho ho ho, merry Christmas!" Do all this in the middle of summer!

Rachel, Drimnagh

A: This doesn't sound like it would be the worst dare in the world, in fact it sounded like it would be quite fun. So what we decided to do, just to make it slightly more interesting, was to carry it out in that lovely little quiet village just outside of Dublin City called Ballymun.

So dressed up as the Jolly Fat Man himself we set off in my bashed up old Peugeot 306, Damo in the passenger seat filming and me driving as Santa. It was a hot summer's day (19 degrees!) and it all started swimmingly. We drove around the flats and streets with Jingle Bells at full volume and as an added treat, just in case I didn't look paedophilic enough, I also handed out sweets to the kids and let me tell you, in Ballymun they do not live by the 'Don't take sweets from strangers' rule.

So we drove around until suddenly Damo spotted a street party happening down a side street.

"Head down there, there are loads of kids, it'll be amazing..." So we did. It looked like it was going to be brilliant fun and we'd enjoy it – ah how naïve we were in the early days of daring.

Within seconds we realised it was a dead end. Even though we're tough and scared of nothing (convinced?) we decided we should do a u-turn anyway. But let me tell you this, the kids in Ballymun are clever and they can adapt to any situation. As the car turned slowly around and we inched back up the road we realised that they had formed a human chain around the car and we were unable to leave.

Sensing our fear they began to chant: "WE WANT SWEETS! WE WANT SWEETS!" They had the car surrounded. On my side there were about 25 kids all shouting in the window and on Damo's side there was one kid staring in at Damo. This is the clever kid. All the others are thinking "Hey we could get free sweets here" while he is thinking "You know how many sweets I could buy with that expensive video camera".

As the shouts got louder and louder, I started to panic. I reached into the Christmas stocking that we had filled with sweets and realised that it was reaching dangerously low levels of sugary goodness. I frantically tried to think of how I was gonna break this to the hordes of already sugar-filled kids who were reaching a bit of a frenzy. In a complete moment of madness I turned the stocking upside down to dump the remaining sweets out. Only at the last second did I realise my mistake. As the sweets fell onto my lap, loads of kids' hands dived for my crotch. The parents' looks of joy turned to horror as they thought a nice treat for their kids had turned into a very elaborate pervert trap. Damo did the worst thing of all to compact this: He turned to me with the camera and shouted: "This is gonna be amazing footage man!"

Jesus!

So the sweets are gone but we're still blocked in and so can't move. Cue the helpfulness of a lovely woman who came over to us and said:

"Sure just drive slowly through them, lads, if you hit them it's their own fault."

Now that's parenting.

We should also give a quick shout out to the two kids whose comments we overheard while we were surrounded in the car.

One of the bright sparks in the bunch realised I wasn't the real Santa. His reasoning was that I wasn't wearing the right shoes. That was the only thing wrong with my outfit – I didn't have the right shoes. Not the fact it was the middle of July or I was driving a Peugeot or I was 26 or I had no presents. It was all to do with the shoes...

Also there was a very scary kid who, upon finding out there were no sweets left, expressed his anger by saying:

"Do you know I'm going to chop you're head off."

Always a lovely thing to hear a seven-year-year old kid saying to anyone, let alone the person who provides him with presents every year. See ya in Mountjoy soon, kid.

TRAVEL

I dare ya to buy a dingy, and sail to Monaco (yes, Monaco!) dressed up as Tunisian immigrants!
Shane, Wexford

CAR

I dare ye to open the doors of cars in traffic and get in and sit down. Ask the driver: "Where are we going?"
Philip, Cork

I dare ya to drive around and wait ages at busy traffic lights and watch traffic go mad.
Jack, Enniscorthy

Book in for an NCT with a go-cart.
Zoe

I dare ya to start drive-by arguments with random people for a minute and then drive off!!
Shay, Armagh

Drive around a car park and wait until you see someone reversing out of a space. When you do, park right behind them so they can't get out.
Shane, Mayo

In public or in your car where there are others watching (stopped at traffic lights, parked at a convenience store, etc.) play opera music really, really loud and head bang.
Mikey

I dare ya to set up a road block at two ends of the same road, trapping motorists in the middle.
Damien, Co Clare

Ok, everyone in Ireland has road rage, especially with van drivers! I dare ya to get into a van and park it in awkward places making it hard for people to get by. Stop and talk to other drivers in vans going the other way while drivers behind you get more and more impatient. Rob someone's parking space and wolf whistle at girls walking by. Drive slowly and take your time at traffic lights! You won't be breaking the law – I don't think!
Karen

D: We'll soon find out!

LUAS AND DART

Get on the LUAS (preferably the red line) in your civvies and demand to see people's tickets (posing as an inspector). See their reactions and more importantly, how many people actually have tickets.

Brenda, Kilmainham & Craig

When you're on the LUAS and people start talking, tell them to "Shhhh!" or "Be quiet!" I thought of this one when I was on the LUAS and the thought of it kept making me laugh out loud so I looked mental.

Aodhagan, Kildare

I dare ya to get a live chicken onto the LUAS and let it go.

Conor

D: The chicken would probably get fined for not having a ticket.

Right so! Drink five litres of water, then, without a toilet break, get on the DART at Greystones. Travel the entire journey to Howth without getting off in between. Insert evil laugh here!!

Bar Aston, South Dublin

Get on a packed DART heading into town during morning rush hour smelling of fish and begin singing along with music on your mp3 player/radio.

Ronan, Dublin & Stephen, Lucan

We dare ya to pole dance on the DART at rush hour, wearing the full gear – tassels, hot pants and thigh high boots.

Aoife & Russell, Arklow

I dare ye to get two sheep and shepherd them onto the LUAS for as long as you can.
Mike

Get on the DART during rush hour. Bring a football with you and play a football match. Steal people's jackets for goal posts.
Ciaran, Dublin

Get onto a DART at rush hour and make a bed in the middle of the carriage. If anyone asks you to move, offer them a place in the bed.
Ciaran, Blanchardstown

On a packed train you receive a phone call from your girlfriend who's about to dump your sorry ass. You don't take it too well at all and in front of the very packed train you plead with her not to dump you. The more desperate and loud you sound the better. Midweek around 5.30pm should do the trick.
Tony, Dun Laoghaire

I dare ya to give flowers and a thank you card to every rude person on a train, especially 'the gentlemen' who won't give up their seat for a lady and those others who barge their way through and make Dublin not nice to be part of – start a revolution in manners.
Peter, North County Dublin

BUS-TED

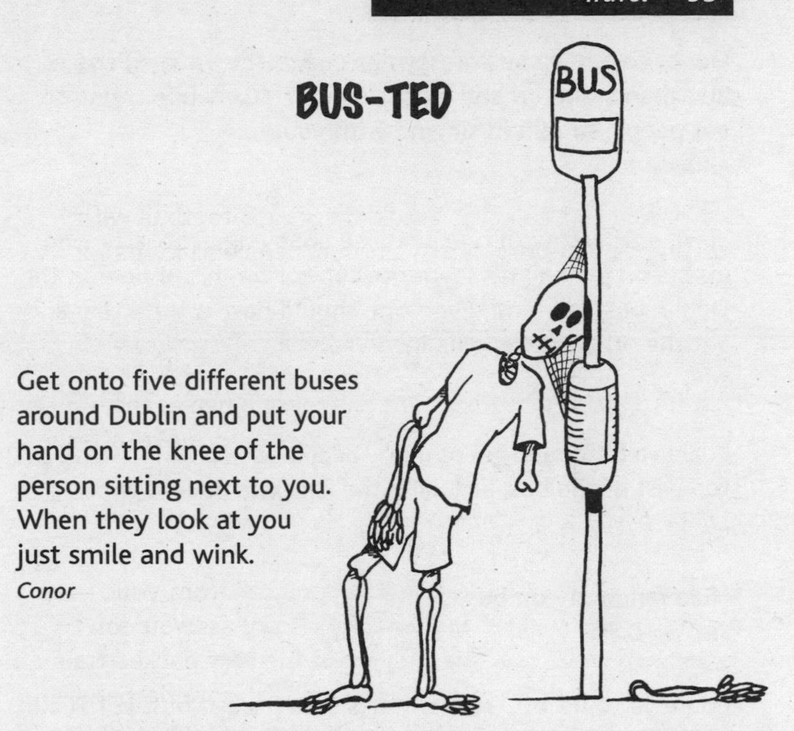

Get onto five different buses around Dublin and put your hand on the knee of the person sitting next to you. When they look at you just smile and wink.
Conor

Get a printed cardboard cut-out of a bus, attach it to the front of your car and drive down the bus lane in rush hour traffic.
Ciaran, Dublin

I dare ya to get on a bus and pay for a family ticket but only use 1 cent coins.
Aaron, Dublin

I dare ye to walk in front of a Dublin bus at traffic lights on O'Connell street. Pretend to faint when you pass the bus, causing chaos and a rather comical situation.
Sean, Ceatharlach

D: Yes, comical indeed...

Get onto a busy bus dressed as one of the Village People and then stand up and start singing YMCA while trying to get people to join in singing with you.
Amanda

Have a DJ war with one of those annoying little g*ts who insists on playing his favourite tunes from his phone on the Dublin bus. Tell him: "Everyone should have a turn." Try and get the other passengers involved.
Bob

I dare ya to try and get as many people as you can to leave the top part of the bus, including the knackers down the back.
Charlie, Dublin

Hula randomly on buses.
Stephen, Dublin

I dare ya to let off loads of farts on a packed bus. LET IT RIP LADS...
Shane, Cobh

I dare ya to have a w*nk on the back of the no. 16 bus.
Conor, Rathfarnham

D: Does the 16A count?

Get on a bus behind a girl (or a guy would be funnier) with long hair and start playing with their hair.
Brian, Trim

TRACTOR

Ah c'mon! There had to be one tractor dare!

Drive around Dublin city centre / M50 in a tractor with a bale of hay at rush hour and ask the thickest Dub for directions to Cavan.
Cian

LET'S FLY, LET'S FLY AWAY...

I dare ye lads to dress up as pilots and go to Dublin Airport. Pretend to be drunk as you stumble through a queue of passengers explaining to them that it is imperative you get to the plane as you are about to fly them to their destination... This is for the Aviator lads in Sligo...
Declan, Sligo

I dare ya, during a flight, to crouch down in the emergency position and wake up the passenger asleep next to you!
Chris Godfrey, Cork

I dare ya to walk into the airport with bags of flour taped to your chest (with your shirt off).
Devereux, Wicklow

Walk into the airport with a ticking suitcase.
Emmet, Wicklow

I dare ya to go to Dublin Airport dressed up as a bird (say a ridiculously large eagle or 'Big Bird' outfit) and queue up for your flight with your luggage, pretending to fellow passengers that you're going to use the airport's runway to depart on your holidays. You can spend time in Departures

limbering up and consuming energy drinks for the flight you are about to embark on!
Alan

I dare ya to stand in the arrivals hall at Dublin Airport and carry out emotional reunions with strangers.
Dee

Book a flight. One of you get into a suitcase, let the other check it in and see how far you can get through the airport in the suitcase before you are stopped!
Paul, Dundalk

I dare ya to set up a Polish welcoming service in Dublin Airport. Hand out leaflets and tell them to head to the West of Ireland (Connemara) where there are loads of jobs.
Mark, Mullingar

Put an empty box with a 'Fragile' sign through the luggage security x-ray in an airport and say it's your great-granny's soul or something and see how they react!
Caoimhe, Clonakilty

Ryanair baggage allowance! I dare ya to wear as many kilos of clothing as you can and then attempt to check in to a Ryanair flight (when I say as many as you can, I'm thinking Michelin Man wandering through the airport). Remember to also pack your bag with your 15kg allowance!
Morgan, Dublin

I have to say I am totally p*ssed off with all this security and baggage nonsense at airports. Only one bag allowed and you must show the whole world what medication you are on in those lovely re-sealable transparent plastic bags. This is, of course, after you manoeuvre your way past Kaska "Did you pack this bag yourself?" Walensa at the Ryanair check-in desk. I dare you two boys to turn up at a Ryanair check-in desk at Dublin Airport dressed only in a pair of Speedos and flip-flops. Just tell 'Kaska' that you are travelling light and don't want to cause any delays at security! I Dare Ya!
Dave, Maynooth

Right lads, here's the dare. I want Andrew to go into any travel agent in the city dressed as a Hobbit (love the hairdo!) from *Lord of the Rings*. You are looking to book flights to Mordor. Right lads, now here's the tricky bit, you have to try and convince the travel agent that Mordor exists so you will need a map printed up as proof! (Sure it's beside Gondor and Rohan.) You will also need a plain gold ring which Andrew must constantly rub

in his hands and refer to as his 'precious'. I bet you a tenner you won't last ten minutes without getting the boot! Good luck!
Karl & Louise, Dublin

TAXI

Flag down a taxi from the opposite side of the road. When he has pulled in ask him if he has the right time.
Kevin C & Dean, Dublin

Flag down a taxi and get in. When the taxi man asks you where to, say here and get out without any other word said.
Jules, Nigel & Josh, Co Tyrone

Get into a taxi and tickle the driver with a feather.
Adrian, Co Clare

Dress up in a KKK suit and wave down a taxi; see if any taxis take you.
Healy, Waterford

I dare ya to annoy a taxi driver to the point where he/she will kick you out of the car.
Conor, Dundalk

DIY TAXI

Drive around Dublin joining taxi ranks. Your taxi sign will be made from cardboard with thick marker pen. I dare ya to get up the noses of some head-the-ball taxi drivers.
Mark

D: This became the most internationally famous dare we did. Very enjoyable too!!

Day 1: Andrew 'borrowed' his Mum's green Fiat Punto and using our art and craft skills, we fashioned a large cardboard sign saying 'TAXI' with thick black marker, glued it to a magnet which stuck onto the car roof very well. To get into the taxi driver frame of mind we didn't shower and riled ourselves up about politics. We were ready for the ranks.

There are an awful lot of taxis out there fighting for a fare. Unless it's Friday or Saturday night there's not enough work for all of them. Some taxi drivers cruise along in great spirits, listening to music and enjoying life but some taxi drivers have a temper shorter than a lesbian's haircut. They're the fun ones.

We each took turns in pulling up to the Stephen's Green taxi rank around the busy lunchtime period. Andrew went first and I hid behind the phone boxes on the corner and laughed at the onlookers pointing at our homemade taxi. Most of the taxi drivers thought it was hilarious. They took photos with their phones and chatted with Andrew or I in good humour.

But the dare said 'get up the noses of some head-the-ball taxi drivers'.

We knew it was coming, we just had to wait.

When we would reach the top of the rank, people

would actually get into our fake taxi. We'd drive them around the block and back to a proper taxi. Then we'd join the back of the rank again.

The only trouble we came into was when a Garda leaned into the window when I was in the rank and said: "What you are doing is illegal and I'm going to have to ask you to leave the rank." I offered him that day's newspaper as a bribe but we both agreed the Page 3 girl was 'muck' so he turned the offer down.

Day 2: As we had such a good time the day before with no real negative response we had to give it another go. It didn't take long today as straight away the vibe wasn't as welcoming as the day before. Taxi men were getting out of their taxis and conferring angrily with each other while glaring over through my windscreen. As I could see them staring I took a swig or two from my naggin of vodka filled with water we'd prepared earlier. That was the last straw and three of them approached my window.

I got an earful of abuse. I was quite amused and also thought to myself 'So that's a head-the-ball taxi driver'. They called the Gardaí on me but I still made it to the front of the rank. Despite the roarings of another taxi man: "He's not a real taxi!" a young woman hopped in the back and we left the rank.

We made it 200 meters down the road before I heard the siren. I pulled over and one male and one female Garda got to work. When he realised it was a prank he asked: "Were you the ones who clamped the clampers in Fitzwilliam Square the other day?"

"Yeah, that was us," I told him.

With a smirk on his face the Garda replied: "We heard about that."

Meanwhile, (I've always wanted to write a story with 'meanwhile' in it) unbeknownst to us, someone took a couple of photos while we were chatting with the law. We arrived back in the production company office 15 minutes later and there was already an email going around of a photo of our dare. The photo featured our dodgy cardboard taxi sign and a squad car immediately behind it with close talks between some guy in a cream jacket and two officers. No one knew we were involved; it was just a random joke on office rotation. The heading was 'Seen on Dawson Street today'. It didn't take long for a bit of racism to creep in. Three weeks later the exact same photo was circling the World Wide Web with the heading 'Romanian Taxi Driver.'

Since that went out we've heard news of the email appearing in inboxes all over America, the UK, other parts of Europe and Australia. We didn't, nor did anyone we know, send any of them! If we learned Romanian at least we could get a job as a famous taxi driver.

SPORTS

I dare ya to cycle from the most easterly point in Ireland to the most westerly one.
Sean, Raheny

D: I looked it up and not including islands, the most easterly point is Burr Point, Co Down and the most westerly is Dunmore Head, Co Kerry. Last one there is a rotten egg!

I dare ya to go ice-skating and deliberately mill in to people and take them out of it!!
Aisling, Foxrock & Rachel, Dublin

I dare ye to go ice-skating in the nip at a public rink!
James, Cork

D: Oooh, you wouldn't want to slip. At least it'd be that cold a bloke's doodle would be tucked in and safe.

I dare ya to use those office chairs with the wheels on the bottom as scooters/skateboards and skate around in public, maybe even go down to a skate park! Wear helmets, wrist, elbow and knee pads, mouth guards, and any other safety gear you want.
Tom, Australia

FEEL THE BURN

Go into a gym, dress up as an overweight person in really tight clothes, bring a packed lunch of fried chicken with you and eat it while you're on the treadmill.
Stephen, Dublin

We are members of Curves Gym. It's a ladies gym. Your dare, should you choose to accept it, is to pose as a woman and try and join this gym...
Jenny & Sarah, Dublin 2

A: No way girls!!! Then we would have to use the same dressing room as females and we all know girls have cooties.

So which one of you two can drink the most amount of water in the least amount of time? You must then do various aerobic exercises, or stand in front of a fountain or anything which would make you go to the toilet. The winner is the person who can last the longest without going for a pee.
Gary, Carlow

Go to a gym and laugh at people working out. Ten points if you get battered.
Joe, Dublin

WHAT GOES UP...

Climb Carrantoohill in the Mcgillicuddy Reeks with one of you wearing a ballerina costume and the other wearing a stripper/hooker costume.
Evan, Co Kildare

A: See that's the sad thing about Ireland's 'mountains'. You could very easily do this dressed in a costume as they're so tiny. Now Everest!!!! That would be extreme fancy dress.

Skydive Mary Poppins style (ie using an umbrella!) Obviously you'd have to have parachutes or whatever!
Shona, Waterford

D: It would be great if by fluke you landed in the driveway of a house where two disobedient brats lived.

I dare ya to tie a kite to your back and run around the Phoenix Park trying to get people to fly you up to the sky. Tell them you've always wanted to be a pilot.
Peter, Finglas

I dare ya to use sellotape to stick yourselves halfway up the spire.
Ronan

Jump off a cliff with faulty bungee gear.
Bob, Cork

D: You can only do that dare the once.

I dare ya to go to a yo-yo competition with a scissors and just start cutting strings. They'd go mad!
Pedro, Laois

GET WET

I dare ya to swim down the Liffey with children's rubber armbands on and a rubber ring.
David & Rachel, Meath & John, Lucan

Let's see the boys race the Liffey from the Ha'Penny Bridge to O'Connell Bridge on surfboards in G Bangers and painted with the national flag.
Scott & Mary, Blanchardstown

I dare ya to canoe around the lake in UCD dressed as swans.
Kirsten

A: That means we could break peoples arms. That's what swans do, right?

I dare ya to get a small rubber boat and dress up like refugees trying to get into the country. Row the boat into a harbour like Dublin or Rosslare.
John, Wexford

Organise a feat of super-human athletic ability that's really not. In typical 'swim the English channel' style have a press conference and get a safety boat, a bull horn, and plenty of cameras and banners. Announce that you're going to attempt to be the first person to successfully navigate the Liffey (from shore to opposite shore).
Adam, Dublin

I dare ya to start taking photos of people in their swimming costumes in a swimming complex –sauna, pool, jacuzzi etc!
Ruth, Galway

Go to the National Aquatic Centre and stand on top of the high board. Say you won't come down until your demands are met. Ask people if they have seen your pet shark/piranha. Take a flutter board and pretend you can't swim. Hit strangers with your flutter board. Sit in front of a water jet, make moaning sounds and say, "Oh yeah... oooh that feels soooo good...." Try to negotiate the price of getting in. Ask small children if they have seen any suspicious-looking sea monsters lately. Ask a nice looking lifeguard to perform CPR on you. Pretend you're drowning.
Maria & Daniel, Dublin 15

A: Holy shit, how many dares can you get into one paragraph in one location. Well done Maria and Daniel!

Live out our childhood fantasies and swim in a swimming pool full of jelly!
Mike

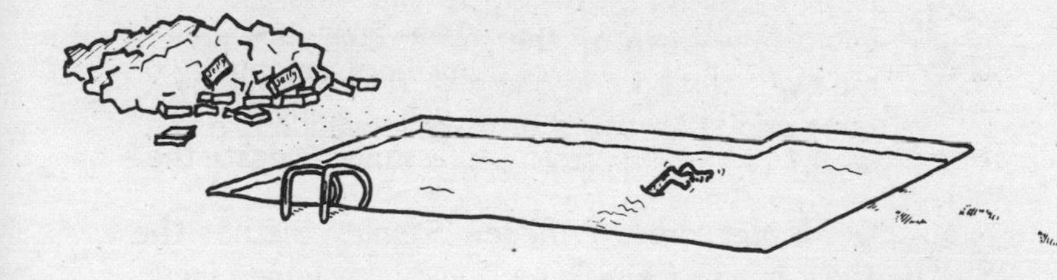

FIGHT!

I dare ya to have a wrestling match in a sports shop and get one of the employees to do the 3 count.
Paulie, Ballyfermot

I dare ya to dress up as sumo wrestlers and have a match in the middle of Grafton Street.
David, Dublin

Join any martial arts school. Make sure you're fully equipped. You need to be already dressed in uniform; either karate, army or a yellow Bruce Lee suit. Have all sorts of sticks, fake swords, nunchucks, anything goes.
Richi, Dublin

Go to the press conference of Wayne McCullough and Kiko Martinez and make a scene shouting that they're both afraid to fight you. You have to talk like Clubber Lang in *Rocky 3*.
Paul, Dublin

A: They would be afraid to fight me! In fact I could take both of them at the same time with me eyes closed and one arm tied behind my back and they could both have weapons and I would still win. Damn straight!

D: Things said by Andrew Stanley are not the thoughts or beliefs of Damo or anyone else here at I Dare Ya Industries.

Provoke someone to fight you but before they do anything, fake a severe injury.
John, Kilkenny

BALLS

I dare ye to slide down a bowling lane and knock down all the pins.
Conor

Go to a fancy golf course and use bowling balls. Play 18 holes.
Billy B.

A: Jaysus I can't even imagine how sore your arm would be after this. I would have to have a week off from, ummmm, making myself happy, if ya know what I mean...

Walk into a sports shop and ask a shop clerk for help. Ask for a basketball jersey, shorts, head sweatband, wrist bands, socks and runners. Try them all on together. When you come out ask how you look and ask for a ball. Dribble it a couple times, then find the nearest basketball net (sports shops usually have portable hoops). Slam the ball in one, turn around and shout out: "Yeah that's the shit, that's the shit, you want some of this punk? Let's play a little one on one or is that why you work here? Because mommy wouldn't let you play sports?"
Liam, Cork

I dare ya to enter an important tennis competition with a set of golf clubs.
Liam, Dublin

Drive a golf ball down O'Connell Street!
David, Galway

RUN!!

Run through a school sports day/sports game in your underpants.
Dermo, Tipp

Right guys, this is kinda a long one. Basically, you need a moped or a bike and jogging gear. You start out in Maynooth where the 66 bus starts its route. As the first people get on, you jog past them. Once the bus passes you out, the other one of you comes behind on a bike. The jogger hops on and every time the bus stops, the jogger hops off and runs past. Basically the people on the bus will think you can jog from Maynooth to town quicker than bussing it!
Sean, Leixlip

D: This is a great one. You could even use doubles dressed in the same gear positioned at bus stops all the way into town, people will think you're the Flash!

I dare ya to run full speed around a corner in Dublin city centre and scream: "RUN!! RUN FOR YOUR LIVES" See how many people run!
Deanie, Laois

D: We gave this dare a good go down Henry Street and Mary Street and no reactions. So we did it numerous times. Bolting through the pedestrians with a crazed look in our eyes and screaming as loud as we could: "RUN FOR YOUR LIVES!!! RUUUNNNNN" Still nothing. People would just glance over and then get back to their shopping. Even if Godzilla himself stuck his head over the Jervis Centre I think the most response anyone would give would be some passersby looking up and saying: "There's that lizard yoke". Then they'd go about their daily business.

We ducked down an alley to catch our breath from just sprinting the length of Henry Street for the sixth time when three teenage boys wanted to get a photo of us. We thought: "Cool! At last people are appreciating our stunts". We both stood upright, chests out and arms over each other's shoulders. The kid with the camera gave us the 'move to the left' gesture with his hand. We obliged. He did it again with a bit more gusto. We budged over a bit more. Then the three of them blurt out in unison: "Move it!" Andrew and I moved completely out of the way to see the sprats take a photo of the graffiti they'd just finished on the brick wall which we were in the way of. How embarrassing. Maybe if we let them spray paint our shirts we'd make it into their photo album.

MORE BALLS

I dare ye to turn up at a football match late and just sit on the bench with the rest of the subs. Apologise for being late and see how long you can stay there.
Paul, Dublin

Go to a children's soccer match and pretend that one of the kids playing is your child.
Eoin, Cork

Erect a small rugby post in somebody's front garden and play rugby.
Conor, Kerry

A: I am glad he said 'rugby post' there...

Go to any junior Sunday league match on a Sunday morning in the Phoenix Park and walk across the pitch during the game dressed as the Pope heading for the Papal Cross.
Eric, Ballymun

I dare ye to go to a hurling match and root for a team that are not playing!
Darren

I dare ya to go to a Dublin GAA match dressed in England shirts and sing *God Save the Queen* during *Amhrán na bhFiann!*
Joe, Dundrum & Joanne, Wexford

Go to a GAA football match and give out to the ref for not spotting all those handballs.
Richie, Dublin

Go to a football match, run onto the pitch and take the ball. Then see how far you can get without getting caught.
Shane, Newbridge & Stephen

I dare the two of you to go to a rugby training session and act as human tackle pads for all the players to tackle and hit!
James, Navan

HILL 16

Go to a Dublin/Meath game and sit in Hill 16 with Meath jerseys on and have 'Hill 16 Scum' printed on the backs of the jerseys!
Gerard

A: We considered putting this one in the No Pain, No Gain chapter as we figured this is what would probably happen: a lot of pain. I honestly don't think I have ever been so terrified of doing anything in all my life. We got our jerseys printed on in a printing store in Stephen's Green Shopping Centre. The people there were more than happy to help us out...hmmmm...maybe we did something that they didn't like us for.

D: Andrew had the idea of adding 'Scum 0' so it looked more like a score board and we might not die. I said we can't add anything to the print, that's not the dare. Andrew goes: 'We're adding zero, which is nothing'. Fair point. Let's do that and we might not end up in a dark room tied to a chair covered in our blood and other people's saliva. With how things panned out, I don't think it really made a difference.

A: So once we had our attire, we headed down to the magnificent Croke Park with worried looks on our faces and a little bit of wee in our pants. Meath wasn't even playing that day! It was Dublin vs Derry. So we were two lost green and yellow wanderers in a sea of blue jerseys. The occasional red jersey was seen from Derry supporters who were also just as appalled at our tops. We had visions of our jerseys becoming red very soon.

We decided to walk along Dorset Street first and see what kind of reaction we got and, let me tell you people, it was instantaneous. People were immediately calling us the worst possible names. Old people started to shout at us that we had 'no respect for the GAA'. The young people seemed to be fine. We soon realised the extent of the pickle we were in when a group of lads told us a heartwarming story about some Meath fans who got their jaws broken while they were standing in the Hill 16 stand. STANDING! Not even wearing the jerseys that we had – just at the game eating their ham sandwiches and Tayto. Holy crap!

Time for us to head down to the Hill and this is where we got the first of our mercies – we weren't allowed film in Croke Park. Thank Christ! Dare abandoned. Time to go home.

What? The producers think we should walk all the way down to the entrance to the stadium anyway? Through all the Dublin fans who will no doubt want to kill us? Why not? We must have done something to them too dammit!

Faces grim, legs feeling like lead, we trudged towards the Park Hill 16 entrance, right through the middle of a sea of blue with every single pair of eyes drilling into our backs through the offensive words. We couldn't even talk. All we wanted to do was run as fast as we could out of there. People begin to shout things.

Small things at first:

"Ya dickheads"
"Do ya wanna bleedin' kickin' or wha'?"
"Jaysus, look at those thicks!"

Then getting more aggressive:

"F**k you ya's pair of pricks!"
"Take that shite off or I'll kill ya!"

And then thank God, and I never thought I would say this, the long arm of the law showed up.

Garda: "What in God's name are ya doing lads?"
Andrew + Damo: "We actually have no idea anymore."
G: "Well, I mean, are ya stupid or what?"
A+D: "Something like that."

At this stage we heard a crackle on the radio and another Garda's voice came on: "Apparently they're wearing some kind of shite on their jerseys about hating the GAA or something. Get them out of there now!"

G: "Sorry lads, but I'm gonna have to ask you to move along before ya start a riot."

I nearly wept.

A+D: "No worries, thanks very much. I think you just saved our lives."

The riot van showed up covered in steel mesh plus six Gardaí and they escorted us out of the entire Croker jurisdiction with jackets covering us as if we just streaked.

Now I am not saying we are wusses but as soon as that happened I know we both felt like hugging that certain member of the law so hard that I am sure we would have gotten arrested for assaulting a Garda.

Thanks for the dare Gerard.

SCHOOL SCHMOOL

Ah good old school days, where the ritual of the dare begins. Good to see some things never change...

INTO DETENTION OR JAIL?

Hijack a school for a day.
Lauren, Westmeath

Break into a school and set the kiddies FREE!!!
Emily, Kildare

I dare ye to go into a school and pose as students. Start blatantly chatting up every teacher – women and men!!!
Jake, Clonmel

Dress in drag and collect a child (preferably one you know) from school.
Sarah, Carlow

Go into a school and claim that the teacher's husband/wife has ordered a stripper for them.
Darryl, Limerick

I dare ya to go to any secondary school and pretend to be students. Any time someone asks you about your age, break down into tears crying: "It's not my fault I'm so stupid."
Fiona, Co Dublin

I dare ya to run through a girls' secondary school at lunchtime – b*llock naked. (Not a primary school, because that would be sick!)
Peter, Dublin & Philip

I dare ya to go into a school and pretend to be a school inspector. Say the school is disgraceful and has to be closed down.
Aidan, Dundalk; Colin, Co Clare; Ralva, Tallaght

I dare ya to go into a school dressed as a Garda and cause hassle.

Jamie Kinnegad, Co Westmeath

Get Andrew to go into his old school in uniform and sit in a classroom with a teacher he used to have.

Pete, Swords

Pretend to be American tourists. Go into a school and take pictures.

Ricardo, Dublin

A: This sounds like something American tourists would actually do.

I dare ya to borrow the campus police car in UCD and take it for a ride while dressed as horses.

Abi & Ami, Sandymount/Ballsbridge

Let a pack of dogs loose in a school.

John, Kilkenny

STUDENT FOR A DAY

Not the funniest dare but we got it from so many young peeps we thought it only fair to mention the dare and all of the darers.

Go back to secondary school and see if you can last the whole day! If there's a female teacher, start chatting her up.

Olivia, Dara & Rachel; Micheal Keating (didn't he play batman?); Kay, Kilkenny; Shane, Skerries; Derek, Shane & Tiffany, Carlow; Stephen, Enniscorthy; Noelle, Kerry; Robyn, Athlone; Richie, Kildare; Michelle, Co Meath; Sinead, Bundoran, Co Donegal; Katieann, Cork; Katie, Tralee; Ryan, Co Kerry; Ronan, Castleknock; Aidan, Melanie, Tallaght, Dublin; Fintan, Dublin; Niall, Shankill; Steph, Louth; Rob, Co Kildare; Cian, Newbridge; Jack, Wicklow; Aoife, Sligo; Jamie, Clondalkin.

TEACHER, TEACHER

Go into a school and pretend to be a substitute teacher and make everyone believe you!

Louise, Thurles; Aine, Cork; Rob, Limerick; Graeme, Navan, Co Meath; Daire, Co Tipperary; Michael, Cork; Cormac, Dublin; David, Glasnevin; Jill, Naas, Co Kildare; Keith, Dublin; John, Dublin; Siobhan, Laois.

I dare you to teach my performing arts class for a day ... and see if you survive!

Sinead, Sallynoggin

D: Cool! Do we get paid?

A: Damo, for actors it is about the love of the theatre not actually the financial rewards you non-thespian you.

COME TO MY SCHOOL!

Please come to my school! Throw cream pies at the teachers.

Louise, Athlone

Please come to my school! And take all the 1st years on a tomato fight.

Marc, Newry

Please come to my school! Be two gay parents and try to enrol a 60-year-old!!

Curtis, Co Donegal

Please come to my school... dressed as teenage girls!!

Keva, Dublin

Please come to my school! Sing 'Barbie Girl'.
Michelle, Co Wexford

Please come to my school! Ask the principal out on a date.
Stephen, Kilcoole, Co Wicklow

Please come to my school! Start dancing with my mate Dave and then do a duet of 'Summer Lovin' from *Grease*.
Shane, Dublin

Please come to my school! St Michaels College!! And run through wearing a Blackrock College jersey and shouting ROCK RULE 66!!!
Paddy, Blackrock

Please come to my school! That's it.
Barry, Tipperary

D: Nice one Barry.

A: Well done indeed Barry. That is genuinely the easiest dare we have ever gotten. Just to arrive at a place and say: "BAM! Dare done!"

THE 'HIST'

D: College gigs are great fun because students are either shy or mad. This combo makes for interesting shows.

This in mind we were invited to perform an I Dare Ya live show in Trinity College, Dublin. Founded in 1592, it's Ireland's oldest and most prestigious university. Should be a hoot!

We kicked off the show in the half-full Ed Burke Theatre to around 200 students. All was kicking along nicely. Showing dares not seen on telly and mucking around with the crowd, it was just how a gig should be.

Little did we realise that at the exact same time just across the Square a serious debate was being held by the oldest undergraduate student society in the world, the 'Hist' (The College Historical Society). The 'Hist' was founded back in 1770 within Trinity College. Every Taoiseach and President of the State has addressed the Society and other notable guests have included Nobel Peace Prize winner John Hume, Reverend Jesse Jackson, Sir Winston Churchill and Senator Edward Kennedy to name a few. We knew nothing about this prestigious history.

The time came in our show to collect dares from the audience. The most popular dare was to go and fetch the Auditor of the College Historical Society, Tim Smyth, and bring him back to the Ed Burke Theatre within a five minute timeline.

Eoin O'Braoin, the head of the Trinity Comedy Society was up for the quest so he, fellow student Cathal Horan and I bolted out of the theatre doors with the cheers of the crowd behind us. Andrew then whipped out comedy gold until our return.

Armed with a camera, Eoin led the way.

"So where is this Tim character?" I asked as we scampered over the cobblestones.

"He's in some debate."

"Cool."

Puffing we arrived at a large varnished door. We pushed the door open and were met with a pin drop atmosphere as hundreds of uprights sitting in a horse shoe formation listened intently to the brown-jacketed speaker. Eyes darted over to us. We smiled nervously and slowly crouched behind some butts in seats. Whispering, Eoin pointed out Tim, who of course was sitting by the end of the table, directly in front of the speaker in the middle of it all. It was clear at that stage that Tim was not going to leave this monumental gathering for our shenanigans.

I whispered to Eoin: "I'll sneak around next to him, ask him to leave with us, you take a photo, we amscray." He nodded confidently. Cathal in the meantime was standing and having a whispering argument with some guy in a grey suit who was trying to kick the three of us out. People started shooshing, it was heating up.

Five minutes was almost up.

I weaved in between the tiny gaps, hitting knees as I go. I dragged the only empty chair I could see over to just behind Tim. The speaker started slowing his speech and our eyes met. I edged forward a bit more. Grey suit caught up with me and he leaned forward and said in my ear: "Security is on their way." I saw the flash go off from Eoin's camera so I turned to grey suit.

"No worries, we're off. Thanks."

As I zigzag back through the annoyed assembly I notice the silence. I think they've stopped! Waiting for us to leave! As I reach the other two misfits, we burst through the door and high tail it outta there.

We can't stop laughing as we skedaddle back to the theatre. I felt like I was a rascal student again. I told them all what happened much to their amusement. No Tim Smyth, but we projected the photo of us with him up on the big screen. Mission not really accomplished, but hilarious. Good night by all.

In the next issue of the *Trinity News* paper, we'd made the front cover with the headline 'RTÉ comedy star invades Hist debate' with the sub-heading 'Damian Clark of "I Dare Ya!" interrupts Hist debate in attempt to abduct Auditor and fulfil dare'. Crikey!

Staff Writer Deirdre Robertson of *Trinity News* writes "I Dare Ya! comedians Andrew Stanley and Damian Clark seemed to reveal an inter-society feud during their gig in Trinity... one spectator dared Damian Clark to fetch Mr Smyth from the GMB, where he was involved in a debate on Russia chaired by former Taoiseach, Garrett Fitzgerald. Mr Clark headed to the GMB and interrupted the debate but was unable to lure Mr Smyth away, despite even sitting down beside him at one point. He returned to the Burke alone and incorporated the story into his stand-up."

Well I'll be. I guess the moral of the story is 'look before you leap'. No harm done. I hope Russia's OK though.

EVERYONE LOVES ANIMALS

FLUFFY & SCALY THINGS

Have sex with a fish.
Marc

Walk a chicken across the road.
Ronan, Dublin

Go into a shop dressed as a gorilla and rob bananas.
Darren

I dare ya to ride a buckamule.
Thomas, Co Dublin

Dress up as a bear and chase little kids around a park.
David & Luke

Walk into a pet shop and do the *Monty Python* 'Parrot Sketch'.
Ronan, Galway

Dress up in fur coats and hand out leaflets with cute furry animals, promoting real fur and its benefits. (You should probably wear fake fur just to be PC.)
Seamus, Mayo

I dare ya to take a cat to the post office, buy a box and try to post the cat to the lost cat's home. (Remember to stab holes in the box for air and put some kitty litter in it!)
Steve, Balbriggan

Try to bury a pet in a coffin in St Stephen's Green – complete with a priest to say prayers.
Zoe

I dare ya to take a pet rabbit on a lead for a walk down Grafton Street while you're dressed up like a fox and barking.
Naomi, Co Wicklow

I dare ya to set up a stand next to the Fungi office in Dingle, charging €1 per person for the hour to see Fungi the Dolphin... Trust me, this will be the best one ever!
Gary, Top of the Pier, Dingle

ZOO

I dare ya to dress up as a penguin and try to sneak in with the penguins at the zoo.
Eoin, Kildare

Go to a zoo. But run out a few minutes later shouting: "Run for your lives, they're loose!"
David, Cork

I dare ya to go round the streets of Dublin in a gorilla suit and scare the life out of as many people as ya can!
Damien, Co Donegal

SIT BOO BOO SIT. GOOD DOG.

Dress up as dogs, go up behind people and sniff their a*ses.
Anto, Kilkenny

I dare ya to find anyone with dogs and tell them you're doing a survey. Ask them is it ok if you ask their dog a few questions. If they agree, get down on all fours and talk to the dog.
Marie, Clonmel

Dress up as a dog and live like a dog for a day, excreting on walls and such like. Go all around Dublin city and don't stop until you find an owner. Go, chase cats and run free! You bitches you!
Grace, Dublin

Try and sell people shaven rats, pretending they're small dogs.
John, Kilkenny

D: Now that's weird. But I'd say there's a part in all of us who wants to try that.

GIDDEE UP

I dare one of you to w*nk a horse!!
Jim Bob, Wexford

Dress up in a two person horse costume and hold up a busy road!
Carol, Offaly

I dare ya to ride a horse around Grafton Street until the guards catch you!
Colm

I dare ya to sell horse meat at the Galway races.
Michael, Dublin

My dare involves one of the lads and a horse. I dare ya to go to the port in Dun Laoghaire on horseback with a walk-on passenger ticket to Liverpool. When they tell you that the horse can't be brought onto the ferry, tell them that the horse is running in some track in England the next day.
James

Go to a hunt with a donkey, saddle up, and join in the hunt.
Declan, Co Clare

D: Tally ho!

BAA & OINK

We dare ya to shag ten sheep in a minute.
Bobby & Brian, Meath

I dare ya to run around Dublin dressed as a goat.
Danny, Mayo

Grease up three piglets and paint 1, 2 and 3 on them. Release the lil buggers in any building or compound of your choosing.
Jezza, Sydney

I dare ya to brush the teeth of a pig.
Jacinta, Mayo

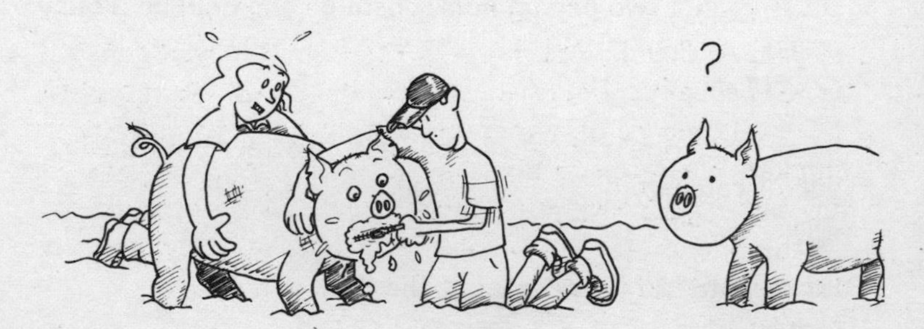

HAVE A COW

Try to milk a very cross cow.
James

I dare ya to lie under a cow's legs, with your face directly under it's a*se and wait until it sh*ts on you.
Mick, Limerick

Go to a cattle mart dressed up in a good suit and arrive in a big limo or some fancy car. Start talking to the people in a posh D4 accent about the cows.
Francis, Monaghan

I dare ye to commandeer some cows from a farm in Westmeath and ride them like you would a horse, round the field. The country air would do ye good!
Niamh, Dublin

Well lads, I dare ya to spend the day on a farm acting like cows, doing everything cows do... eating grass, pooing (only if ya need to) and being milked. (Carry a pouch with milk in it!)
Samantha

WHO YOU CALLING CHICKEN?

Eat KFC in front of a live chicken and stare at it intently.
Anna, Dublin

A: Cruel? Yes. Funny? Yes. I felt it was fairly cruel as I'm a vegetarian and so we had to get Damo to be the one who was going to eat the chicken We tried to hire out some chickens for the day but I guess we must have sounded kind of dodgy on the phone as they wouldn't let us take a few chicks out for the day. Go figure.

We carried this dare out in Edinburgh. We did a bit of research and found a lovely place called Gorgie City Farm and so armed with KFC Chicken burgers and buckets of chicken, we headed on down.

We couldn't find any chickens initially as it was close to closing time. We couldn't ask for help because of course if you work in a place like that you probably aren't going to let some idiots treat the animals in a mean way. So we snooped around in the barn and eventually found some chickens high up on a perch that was behind a fence. We started jumping up but only ended up scaring the life out of them. Then Damo nearly got his burger eaten by a crazy burger loving cow named Bunty.

Just when we thought we weren't gonna be able to do it, and Damo would be eating greasy goodness for nothing, we spotted, hidden in the corner, a coop with a white, feathery chicken inside. So we grabbed the chicken out and Damo wolfed down one of his lovely cousins right in front of him. To be honest the chicken didn't look too perturbed. Who are we to judge? Maybe his cousin did something really mean to him when they were chicks and so he was glad he was getting his just desserts. Just to be as cruel as we could, after finishing his meal Damo picked up the chicken, placed him in the large KFC bucket and carried him out of the farm. Yum!

LET'S GO SHOPPING!

Shopping is one of those daily jobs that people all over the world are doing. This seems to have inspired people to come up with a massive array of ideas to spice up their chores.

Go to a busy shopping centre, run up to a randomer and jock them.

John, Sligo & Ruth, Kildare

Go to Argos and keep taking out catalogues until you can build a castle of catalogues in the street outside.

Conor, Limerick

Go to a busy shopping centre. Pretend to be a gay couple, approach people and offer to buy their children. Say that you can't afford to go to Africa like Madonna or Angelina Jolie but you'll be damned if you're missing out on this fashion trend.
Anna

I dare ya to go into pharmacies and ask the assistants if they can fit you for condoms...
Shane, West Cork

A: That would be extra large for me anyway, ladies...

Go to a supermarket and shout at the people working there till you find out where the "Jizz" (this does not exist) is.
Kevin, Cork

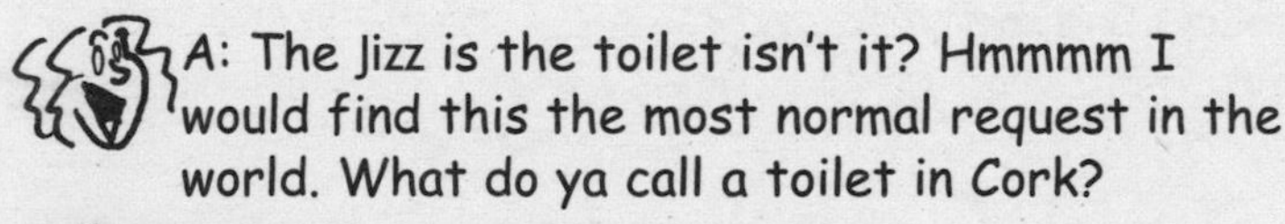

A: The Jizz is the toilet isn't it? Hmmmm I would find this the most normal request in the world. What do ya call a toilet in Cork?

D: I believe Jizz is also a word for population paste.

MANNEQUINS

Go into a big department store and start beatin' up the mannequins.
Daniel, Rathfarnham

I dare ya to go into a women's clothes shop and feel the tits on the mannequins.
Kev, Meath

I dare ya to go into a busy department store and find a female mannequin and slap her in the face and say: "You slept with me and never called me back!"
Nicole, Wexford

Climb into the window displays of shops and pose for as long as you can before getting caught.
Conor, Balrothery

BABY SEAT

I dare ya to go to a supermarket and act like a spoilt child. (Take stuff off the shelves and throw it around the shop.)
Robert, Galway, Karen & Ellen, Jimmy

I dare ya to go into a supermarket and jump into people's trolleys and say: "Mammy/Daddy I want this!!" And start putting stuff into their trolleys!!!
Aine, Tipperary

Go into a shopping centre wearing just a nappy. Then go up to people and tell them you have lost your mother and ask them if they have seen her.
Edel, Tullamore

Both of you to go into a supermarket. One must dress like a baby and sit in the trolley. The second must dress like a woman and do the shopping. Wearing a nappy is optional.
Karl, Balbriggan

D: At least we get the option, thanks Karl.

Get a kid's toy laser gun type thing that makes loads of noise when you pull the trigger. Go around jumping out and surprising people with it in a supermarket or somewhere like that.

Luke, Dublin

I dare you guys to go into a kid's shop and pretend you're five years old and wreck the place to see how long it takes to get thrown out by security. (They never throw anyone out. Ever!) It's a kid's shop so the kids can play with whatever they want, and the staff are not allowed to give out to children... Go on, see how long you last.

Louise, Co Dublin

FUN WITH TROLLEYS

I dare ya to pay a euro for a shopping trolley and try selling it for more.

Alan, Ratoath

A: Sounds like Alan is an amazing entrepreneur.

I dare ya to go to a supermarket and do your shopping, not from the shelves, but from other peoples' trolleys!!! They haven't paid for them so it's not theft, but I'm sure they'll be p***ed off!

Conor, Mallow; Grace & Adam, Dublin; Ronan & Alanna , Tralee; Tony, Kerry; Patrick, Ballinasloe; Ted, Cork; Rob, Portarlington.

D: Phew! A few peeps sent that one in.

Fill up two shopping trolleys with ice-cream and go to the till. When the person is ringing up the ice-cream say: "I forgot the milk." Then ditch the trolleys and don't come back.

Vincent

Spend a day offering to help people with their shopping, if they say no... insist. If they say yes, examine their shopping and ask why they buy things that are bad for their body, soul, mind, the world etc.

Olivia, Sligo

I dare ya to have a shopping trolley race through a shop with random people's shopping trolleys.

Darren, Sligo

Go around a busy street in Dublin with a dildo in your pocket. Have it 'accidentally' fall out in front of people and make awkward situations. (Maybe a Garda Station, post office, bank, oh and around Tesco, throwing dildos in people's trolleys...)

Josef

I dare ya to go into a supermarket and fill two trolleys. Wait until all the shopping is put through the till, then just run out of the shop... leaving some poor unfortunate the fun of putting it all back... ha ha ha!

John, Offaly

D: That's quite an evil laugh you have there John.

I dare ya to push your buddy from Dublin north city limits to Dublin south city limits in a shopping trolley. (No extra padding or lawn chairs allowed.) On the way back, trade spots, from south city limits to north city limits.

Kevin, Meath

SECURITY!

I dare ya to go into Dunnes Stores wearing Tesco uniforms and hand out Tesco offer pamphlets trying to persuade customers to leave Dunnes and do their shopping at Tesco instead.

Paul & Caroline, Tipperary

Dress up as a security guard in a shopping centre and kick people out for no reason. See how long it takes the normal security guards to cop on to you.

Gavin, Drogheda

I dare ya to pretend to be ticket inspectors in a tiny elevator in a shopping centre or some place.

Aoife, Dublin

I dare ya to stand outside a shop/supermarket and pretend to be a bouncer only letting women and children into the shop.

Darragh, Galway

DOES MY BUM LOOK BIG IN THIS?

I dare ya to go into a busy shopping centre and start trying on clothes in public. Ask strangers what they think and 'do you think my bum looks big in this?' etc. Then tell them that you think it would look better on them...

Miriam, Donegal

Have a hippie fest in St Stephen's Green Shopping Centre! Medallions and peace pipes all round!

Dan and Kev

I dare ya to dress up as Superman and go shopping.

Paul, Cork

Walk around a shopping centre dressed as Indians, looking for your tribe!!

Grace, Dublin

I dare ya to dress up as a clown and go into a shop and juggle items for as long as possible.

Robbie, Co Mayo

I dare ya to walk through the Blanchardstown Shopping Centre in thongs – one horse thong and a Santa one.
Ellen, Finglas

I dare ya to walk around a shopping centre in your boxers with no trousers on and ask random people if they have seen jeans anywhere!!!
David, Bray

I dare ya to go to a big shopping centre and go swimming – in Speedos – in the pools and fountains they have there to collect money for charity!
Donnchadh, Ennis

Enter Dublin's busiest supermarket. Put on a builder jacket and hot pants and start packing shelves.
Jack, Cork

I dare ya to run through Dundrum Shopping Centre in a mankini.
Alex, Wicklow

I dare ya to dress up as a nurse and set up a stall outside a supermarket. Offer free on-the-spot colostomies.
Peter, Ballyboughal

Run through a shopping centre wearing just a thong...That would be brilliant and comical.
David, Ireland

Dress up as fairies and go shopping in the city centre.
Orla, Wicklow

Dress up as a bush in St Stephens Green Shopping Centre and jump out at random people.
Sean, Longford

Dress up as a ballerina and then go shopping in Superquinn in Blackrock on a Saturday morning. Keep asking for advice from fellow shoppers.
Adam, Dublin

I dare ya to dress up like someone from *Fame* or the *Call On Me* video (the clothes have to be blood-stopping tight) and get one of the small trampolines. Go into a shop with jamming tunes and try to get shoppers to join in with your workout.
Emily, Skerries

A: This is truly one of the oddest dares we ever received:

I dare ya to go into Tesco dressed as old fashioned boxers with fake mustaches. Put a chicken on each hand and then do fisticuffs down the aisle.
Dale Robinson, Caboom

I WANNA ROCK!

I dare ya to walk into a musical instrument shop, pick up a guitar, play it and then smash it off the ground like Jimi Hendrix.
David, Mayo

Stand in the middle of a shopping centre and sing a song at the top of your voice. The song can be your choice! :)
Eimear, Co Clare

A: Aww thanks for the choice Eimear, you're so sweet... supermarket karaoke sounds like lots of fun!

Play a gig in an 'air' band (as in air guitar) in a shopping centre.
Lukas

CHECK OUT THE CHECKOUT

Return clothes that you have bought with the tags still on... while wearing them!
Ash, Offaly

Go into a shop and get something that costs €2.50 and take out a fiver. Cut it in half and give them half of it.
Ciaran, Westport

We dare you to go to Tesco and get ten packets of headache tablets, five bottles of gin, a rope, a set of sharp knives and a packet of razors. Go to a cashier and see if they will sell you the lot.
Evelyn & Ciara, Wexford

Go into a pharmacy and buy some Sudocrem. Then leave and come back 15 minutes later with it smeared all over your face and neck. Ask to speak to the pharmacist and say you're concerned that you may have overdosed on Sudocrem and ask for his advice.

Tomas

Hey boys, got a funny one for you. I dare you to go to a supermarket and have only one purchase. Make sure to queue up at those checkouts where all the mums have huge trolleys full of stuff. When you get to the till, take out a pocket full of coppers 1c, 2c and 5c coins to pay for the item. Make sure you make obvious mistakes and start over the counting progress again and again to try to get up the noses of all those rushing mums queuing behind you!!

Eve, Cork

Go on a huge shopping spree and try and pay for stuff with monopoly money. (One thing to do would be to try and buy a really expensive car...)

Shona, Waterford & Ciaran, Limerick

I dare ya to try and rent a movie by using gay bribes instead of money.

Tommy, Dublin

Go into any supermarket and fill your trolley to the top with alcohol, spirits, lager, wine, etc... Then get a packet of nappies and put them on top of the drink. Go to the checkout counter. When the person gives you the total amount you have to pay, let on that you don't have enough money. Ask her to deduct the nappies from the price and watch for what will hopefully be a great reaction.

Kevin, Clare & Donners, Co Kildare

I dare ya to go into a supermarket and see if there are any tills with no one at them. Then go to that till and start scanning food and charging people really high prices.
Aoife, Dublin.

I dare ya to go to a 24 hour garage at night and ask through the window for the largest cucumber they have, four packs of condoms, baby oil, Vaseline, a pair of marigold gloves and a jumbo pack of toilet roll. Do all this dressed in drag.
Moritz, Limerick

Return a dildo to a sex shop asking for a refund – say it doesn't fit.
Shane, Limerick

Walk into a second hand charity shop and ask them would they take 'used condoms'. Put cream in the condoms to make it look like... well you know!!
Eoin, Gorey, Co Wexford

D: Gross, but effective.

One of the most annoying things for me is to see people jumping the queue, so I dare ye to spend part of a day jumping the queue without asking or giving a reason. Good luck.

Anna, Cork

Walk into a very busy supermarket/shop/waiting room and blatantly jump the queue. When people get mad, tell them your imaginary friend was minding your spot and you MUST act very insulted when they ask!!

Eugene, Co Kerry

I dare ya to go into a store such as Aldi or Lidl with a Tesco product and attempt to purchase that item.

Brian, Waterford

Go to the GPO and ask do they sell gay Polish ostriches!

Aislinn, Galway

D: This next one is a must try, especially around St Valentine's Day...

Well lads, I dare ya to go into any shop that sells Playboy, the men's mag. Pick up a copy. Also pick up a box of tissues. Then pick up a bottle of hand lotion. Go to the counter to pay for all these items (make sure a hot girl's serving you). Just before you pay, say: "Oh, might not need this stuff." Then ask her out on a date! When she says no, which she will, just say: "No problem love, will defo take them so." It will be epic!!

Stephen, Monaghan

FIVE FINGER DISCOUNT

I dare ya to take two chairs into a supermarket and sit at the salad bar. Eat straight from it and see how long it takes before someone asks you both to leave!

Leah, Louth

I dare ya to go into a supermarket and pick up as many items of food as you can. Eat them and when you're finished, bring up all the empty packets and pay for them.
Ryan, Co Offaly

A: There's nothing daring about that, is there? That's just a normal shopping trip...

I dare ya to go into a local supermarket and go to the aisle where all the tins are. Remove some labels and change them with labels from other tins, ideally done with tins of dog food and tins of beans, it's quite funny.
Edel, Co Dublin

I dare ya to go into a shopping centre and help yourself to some food and drink. Then have a picnic on the floor of the shop and get shoppers to join you. Invisible friends welcome.
John, Belfast

I dare ya to go into five toy stores and ride the bikes out of the shops.
Rita, Galway

I dare ya to go around Dunnes and eat food from each aisle, leaving trails of food around the shop... then leave the shop exclaiming that you're full!
Fiona, Dublin

I dare ya to try to return a cooked, half eaten chicken to Tesco. You bought it raw but you want to return it because it didn't turn out right and you want your money back. Don't take no for an answer. You have to get your money back or be removed by security.
Kevin, Meath

MALLRATS

Live in a 24-hour Tesco for 24 hours or more.
Sean, Co Kildare

Hang around a supermarket all day from first thing in the morning till close and eat breakfast, lunch, dinner, tea and supper there while doing other sh*t as well?
Sean

A: So basically just spend a day in a shopping centre then Sean eh? I wonder how boring your life is that you find that daring...

I dare ya to play dead on a bench or on the ground in a shopping centre. When you're confronted, laugh and point in their faces!!
Michael, Cork

I dare ya to bring a coffin into a shopping centre. One of you has to lie in the coffin while the other pushes the coffin down stairs.
Cormac, Co Down

Snowboard down the escalator in Dundrum Shopping Centre...
Kay, Kilkenny

I dare ya to go into a shop, pick up an expensive item and throw it to a member of staff/customer after shouting "think quick"!!
Noel, Co Meath

I dare ya to walk into a D.I.D Electrical and put microwavable popcorn in a microwave. Cook it in the microwave and then take it out and walk out.
Marko Polo and Alexander the Great

I dare ya to buy a slab of beer cans in a shopping centre and then go into a bar, land them all on the counter and start drinking them as if you were at home!
Jim, Limerick

In a clothes shop hide in a rail between the clothes and wait for somebody to come along. Then pop your head out and shout at them: "Pick me! Pick me! Pick me! Pick me!"
Jenna , Donabate, & Caroline, Roscrea

Get Damo in a wheelchair and wheel him into a supermarket. Damo screams his head off so Andrew gets pissed off and just leaves him there. So Damo is just left in the supermarket screaming his head off.
Kilian

I dare ya to get into two wheelchairs and go to a busy shopping centre. Park the chairs in a disabled parking spot and chain them to a pole or something so that they can't be moved. Get out of the chairs and go shopping, then come back and sit into the chairs. Leave merrily on your way.
Mary, Leitrim

Go into clothes shops and unfold as many things as you can. Make no effort to refold them. Do this until the assistant gets really p*ssed.
Tony, Ratoath

D: A favourite pastime in Penneys...

Enter a shop that has no toilet. Ask the shop assistant if you can use their toilet. Proceed to urinate in your pants when they refuse your request.
Adrian, Templeogue

Go into a shop in just your underwear holding an open bottle of wine. Basically just follow people around slurring stuff like: "I grew cabbage out the back for a couple of years" or "I remember there used to be a pool table round here somewhere" or "Have you seen me keys?"
Fergal, Dublin

D: That's deluded Fergal, but we like it.

I dare ya to go into a local supermarket and take produce from the shelves and make and eat some lunch in the shop. You know the idea, some bread, a plastic knife, some butter and some meat to make a sandwich, maybe a plastic cup of coffee. Ask someone for hot water for the coffee, or the old classic (we've all done it) drink and eat your way through your basket before you reach the check out and only pay for one of those *Take Your Pick* type magazines.
Warren

I dare ya to go to a Tesco Store and set all the alarm clocks in house wares to go off at 5 minute intervals. Move a 'CAUTION – WET FLOOR' sign to a carpeted area and go into a fitting room, shut the door and wait a while ... then yell loudly: "There's no toilet paper in here!"
Anthony, Co Roscommon

Get fake blood and go into a shop and pour it along the floor leading to the ladies toilet. Ha ha.
Chris, Co Cork

PRICE CHECK ON 'RANDOM'

I dare ya to let a rabbit loose in the Whitewater Shopping Centre in Newbridge.
Mark, Newbridge

I dare ya to bring a portabog slapped in Tesco Value labels into a Tesco and try to buy it as a 'Tesco Value Tardis'. Doctor Who and sidekick costumes optional.
Tall Paul

I dare ya to go into a supermarket and get into the freezer. Stay there for 15 minutes while handing customers out their shopping...
Darragh

We dare ya to run around a supermarket screaming at the top of your voice. When someone asks "What's wrong?" say "nothing" and walk out of the shop. See who can get the most people asking them...
Kate & Mary, Balbriggan

I dare ya to walk up behind people in a shopping centre and on a busy street very quietly so they don't realise you're behind them. Scream "I Dare Ya" or something really random at the top of your voice in their ear and see how many people you scare the bloody hell out of!!
PJ, Co. Down

Go out to a shopping centre and talk to yourself and when people look at you weird, run around acting crazy.
Dylan, Cavan

A: Yeah 'cos that will stop them looking at us weird won't it!?

I dare ya to go into an internet shop and watch a porn site on maximum volume.
Kevin, Dublin

Go into a supermarket and bring supermarket products with you such as a pint of milk and tomato sauce. Pretend you're stealing these items and sprint out of the store. When security stops you, you've already bought them in a different store!!
Mark, Monaghan

Walk into any supermarket. Go to the intercom and announce that the next 10 customers that walk out the door with their shopping unpaid will get it for free!!
Eoin, Co Wexford

Create an "Adopt a Baby Vending Machine"; watch people stare in horror. (I have no idea how you would pull this one off, but, oh, if you could!)
Adam, Dublin

I dare ya to go to Liffey Valley Shopping Centre in Lucan and try to make someone think that you are their real father. Even make them ring their mother and ask her!
Monica, Dublin

I dare ya to go into a shopping centre with a handbag. Stand outside a lift until somebody goes into one of them... get in with the person. When the doors shut, open your bag and start talking as if somebody was inside it (like a leprechaun). Say stuff like: "Are you alright in there? Do you want a cup of tea? I can ask this man/woman to get you one if you like?"
Bekky, Co Laois

I dare ya to set up an elocution stand in Ballymun Shopping Centre and ask passersby if they want to learn how to speak properly...
Sinead, Laois

TROLLEY TIPS

Dear lads, I dare ya to go into a supermarket and take someone's trolley full of food and just walk away with it.
Paul, Kilkenny

D: We did the above dare from Paul. We carried it out in Dunnes in Kilkenny itself and we figured out a few things in the process to keep in mind when carrying out such a task.

DO

Look for trolleys carrying a decent amount of groceries. Make it worth your while, plus they would've spent more time on it, therefore you'll get a bigger reaction.

Hold some items in your hand as if shopping yourself, you appear less suspicious.

Remove all handbags and personal belongings of the shopper or you may get a tin of beans in the back of your head.

DON'T

Let the staff see what you're up to or they'll call over the security guard in the black tie and peach collared shirt.

Take the trolley of anyone with large scars or tattoos of tear drops on their face.

Run off with a trolley that has a child sitting in the seat.

THE CRAZY CAROL PAGE!

D: Something tells us Carol wants us to ask out the security guy...

Pretend you're gay and ask the security guard in Tesco in the Square in Tallaght out on a date.
Carol

6 days later:

I dare ya to go to Tesco in the Square and ask the security guard out on a date. Pleeeeeeeeease.
Carol, Ballyfermot

12 Days later:

I dare ya to go to Tesco in the Square in Tallaght and ask the security guard on a date, Gerry if possible, please and thank you.
Carol, Ballyfermot

D: We emailed Carol to see if there's a back story between her and this 'security guard'. She got back to say "He's my hubby and I want to piss him off just for the buzz, thanks."

He's one lucky guy.

AND THE WINNER IS...

Go to a supermarket and sneak boxes of condoms into old people's baskets.
Declan, Manchester

A: This is possibly the best dare we have ever received and one we could easily have spent the whole day doing. It's free, easy and a heck of a lot of fun. So we hit the supermarket armed with 12 pack boxes, lube included, ribbed for her pleasure.

The lovely elderly lady, or 'Target A' as we like to refer to her, didn't notice anything out of the ordinary going through the till. But when she got outside she realised something was up. As soon as she found the condoms, she went straight back in. Of course she went to the customer services desk.

What did they do? With all their training in customer service and dealing with the public you would think they would be able to handle any situation. What a shame then that the manager in question when presented with the predicament of the lady, just burst out laughing. As if that wasn't bad enough, he then called over other staff members to laugh at her as well! Not so much 'the customer's always right', more so 'the customer's freakin' hilarious'.

One thing we have to say is that Declan who gave us the dare was actually a 15-year-old boy, which is funny enough, but when you add in the fact that he was at the show with his grandparents, pure brilliance. We asked Declan where he got this idea that had the audience cheering so loudly. He just subtly pointed to his grandparents, nodded and gave us the thumbs up.

Nice.

MOST REQUESTED DARE

A: The great thing about collecting dares is finding out just what people want to see. What do people find funny?

Well, turns out, the most requested dare was this one:

I dare ya to dress up as a woman/drag queen, then go into a lingerie shop and get yourself measured for a bra and knickers. Ask the assistant: "How do I look? Does my bum look big in this?" Then hit the town and flirt with lots of men.

D: We got this dare and ones just like it from 2,754 people. You know who you are!!

The public has spoken.

Men dressed as women is still one of the funniest things in the world. Better grab my wig and lippie.

HEAD IN THE TOILET

Ewww. Gross. You are so immature if you think any of this is funny. Call us toddlers then.

POO, BUM, BALLS

Eat poo.
Naomi & Hamza, Dublin

D: ...and it's all down hill from here...

Stick your finger up your hole and lick it.
Ian & Phil, Cork

Pour hot candle wax on your balls!!! Have Fun!!
Jean & Christina, Co Mayo

Lick each others balls.
L Baxter, Dublin

To wait till one of your friends falls asleep, then suck his balls and take a pic!
Luke, Wicklow

Get "cock" shaved in the back of your head.
Rob, Dublin

Drink two bottles of laxatives.
Mikey

D: We were going to do the laxative dare, had the bottles and everything but to be safe, rang the doctor for some advice. He said don't do it. "Why not?" we asked. He proceeded to tell us that you'd squirt out your poo at first, that's the funny bit, but then you'll just have excruciating stomach cramps for days and you won't be able to move. So there ya go kids. From the doctor's mouth, don't do drugs or laxatives.

I dare ya to eat dog poo.
Joe, Dublin

I dare ya to try and fart 100 farts in one day.
Deirdre

D: What Deirdre should know is that most men do that anyway.

I dare ya to pour a whole bottle of after shave down your pants.
Darragh, Co. Cork

I dare ya to have a farting competition in a warm confined/close space where there are lots of people around – a lift perhaps. At Mass would be my preference for the craic but methinks you'd go straight to hell for even suggesting it. You must have a good dose of ingredients to make ye windy in the first place.
Nelzer

TWO PLY CAR

Wrap toilet roll around someone's car when they are in it, get on the roof, sing a song and wave a flag...
Eanna, Leitrim

D: We did this one in Carrick on Shannon, well, attempted it. This shows how tight-knit some town folk can be. We bought a family pack of tissue paper in 'Paddy's', had a shiny black Alfa Romeo targeted and an I Dare Ya flag at the ready.

Some giggly school girls saw us, told the shop owner who told the people in the chemist and before we'd wrapped the toilet paper around twice, the car owner was standing at his bonnet tapping his foot with arms folded. What do ya say when you're caught 'rapid'.

"We thought your car woulda looked betta covered in dunny roll," I blurted out. The Alfa Male didn't seem to agree.

So remember, when carrying out a dare where everyone knows everyone, do it unnoticed or to someone they all hate.

SH*T HEADS

Poo in a clear plastic bag and walk around Edinburgh with it stuck to the back of your head.

Sicko girls, Edinburgh

D: We carried out this dare in Edinburgh – not our proudest moment. The one delight was Andrew couldn't 'go' when we needed to so he had to wear my warm poo on his head. Ha ha! That alone made this disgusting dare worth it.

PUBLIC TOILETS

I dare ya to poo in a urinal.

Matthew, Dublin & Ciaran, Cavan

Go into a girl's bathroom and pee in the sink.

Patrick, Swords, Co Dublin

Eat toilet paper.

Robert, Dublin

I dare ya to go into a public toilet with a roll of toilet paper in your hand. When people walk in, ask them if they want their asses wiped!
Jack, Castlebar

Produce a sperm sample in the public toilets in Connelly Station. Go on, I dare ya!
Gareth, Howth

I dare ya to rub crap on yourselves (any kinda crap) and then go shopping.
Shane, Galway

I dare ya to dress up as a woman and walk into a men's public toilet. Stand next to a man at a urinal and lift up your skirt and take a piss!
Sean, Dublin; Eugene, Ballinasloe; Gareth, Enniscorthy

Walk into a girl's bathroom and ask if anyone has a spare tampon.
Chris, Dublin

I dare ya to switch the ladies and gents toilet signs in a public toilet and stand at the urinal and wait for a person to come in...
Dara & Jason, Limerick

Walk into a pub bathroom and talk to some guy having a wee, and comment on his penis's size.
Gavin, Sligo & Brian, Kilkenny

Eat a urinal cake.

Ciaran, Cavan

THE STREETS ARE PAVED WITH POO AND WEE

Take a piss on the spire at rush hour.

Jonathan, Co Meath

I dare ya to wear a shirt with an English flag on it, go into town and pee on the front of the GPO building on a busy day.

Michael, Dublin

Piss in a bag and ask someone to hold it while you tie your shoe. (Make sure the piss is warm.)

Diarmuid, Limerick

D: Follow the yellow wee road.

I dare ya to stick your dick out of a window in a building and take a piss.
Tomas, Co Galway

Urinate in a public swimming pool.
Vincent, Howth

D: Doesn't everyone?

I dare ya to fart in a bottle, close the top and walk up to random people and tell them to open it and smell it.
Jamie, Limerick

I dare ya to go up to ten people and burp in their face!
Diarmuid

I dare ya to stick a toilet plunger to a random bald guy's head. It's great fun! (It doesn't hurt but it does get stuck and it's gas trying to take it off.)
Michael

I dare ya to go up to random girls in Dublin and ask them for a tampon because your friend with a big nose has a bad nose bleed. See if you can get five.
Richie, Bray

I dare ya to do a shit in public.
Calum, Shankill, Dublin & James, Fermoy

Shit on a path, then put it in a bag and put it in a bin.
Daniel, Galway

D: At least Daniel cleans up after himself.

Go around houses asking can you take a massive dump in their house. Make really loud noises while in the toilet if you get in.
Caolan, Dublin

Try and sell genuine leprechaun shit to tourists.
Gareth, Howth

Set up a stall selling your own real poo. Price it by measurement and quality (fibre content etc). Also have bags of runny poo to sell. Try to persuade people to buy them.
Richard & John, Cork

TOILET DUDE

Dress up as a toilet and walk around Grafton Street asking women to sit on you.
Nicola, Portlaoise

A: Sometimes we like to have a go at arts and crafts in our dares and this one was probably the most 'make and do' that we did for all of them. We made a giant toilet out of a big TV box that we covered in white paper and stuck a big lump of plasticine-type stuff sticking out of the corner for a handle. I also wore a full length white one-piece suit and painted my face white just in case people thought I wasn't actually a toilet.

Hitting the streets holding a toilet seat and asking people to sit on you if they want a wee isn't as hard as it seems – it's way worse than that. After a few failed attempts I realised I wasn't getting anywhere fast and we needed another enticement for the ladies to shower me with goodness. Thank God for Tesco. We went in and purchased what all good toilets should have when they are trying to seduce the ladies – a Harpic smelly thing-a-me-jigger! Once I had that the ladies were all over me, sitting on me, hugging me, rubbing me. AMAZING!

D: Andrew also went into Stephen's Green Shopping Centre to use the public toilets, followed close behind by me with the handycam. It's usually 20 cents to use their facilities but toilets get in for free! Money saving tip: If you can be bothered dressing up as a white thunder box, free public toilet use!

Our Toilet Dude sat in a cubicle and waited for a bursting citizen to surprise. This worked quite well as guys stepped into the narrow space and were confronted with: "Hey man, need to go? A one or a two?" We found a mobile phone sitting on the ledge behind the real toilet. After confusing a few blokes who needed to take a dump, a guy with dark hair and in his twenties traipsed in looking for it.

Rattled at the sight of a human toilet, but determined, this guy asks: "Errm, did you see a phone in here?" Toilet Dude hands it to him and booms: "There you go!! I'm not just a Toilet, I'm a Pooper hero!!" Thankful he got his phone, the guy said 'cheers' and ambled out. I often wonder what he told his mates when he returned with his phone.

"Get your phone back?"

"Yeah the toilet gave it to me."

"You mean you found it in the toilet?"

"No, the toilet *gave* it to me."

NO PAIN, NO GAIN

This chapter contains the piercing, tattoo and hair removal dares. There are people who get these done to themselves every day...but that doesn't make them any less painful.

I dare ya to get a tattoo of each other's faces on yisser bums.
Jennifer

STICK METAL IN YA

Get both your butt cheeks pierced together...
Stacy, Laois; Daire, Dublin; Mary, Tallaght

I dare ye to get yer belly buttons pierced!
Rebecca & Caroline, Cork

D: Andrew did this dare and kinda liked it. He kept his shiny stud in his belly button for a good ten months.

To pierce one or both nipples...

Tilda

D: When people ask us what was the worst dare we had to do I always say this one. Andrew and I got both our nipples pierced and it was excruciating. My body was rejecting them from day one. The thing I didn't know about piercing is how much attention you have to give them. Clean them with sea salt and anti-microbial soap. Stuff that. The last thing I want to do with my day is poke around my nips with cotton swabs and germicidal soap. Climbing trees and bumping into things became more uncomfortable than needed. Why would anyone want another reason to not get dirty? Andrew didn't seem to mind them as much but three months later, after the second filming was done, I whipped them straight out. They healed up without a trace of intrusion within a week. I guess I'd make a terrible cyborg after all.

For Damo to get his nipples pierced...again!

Daire, Galway

D: No! Anything but that.

Each of you get your nipple pierced, then link your piercings with a chain. Walk down the street and try to catch people in between you so they get caught in the chain... go on ... it'll be gas!
Graham, Dublin

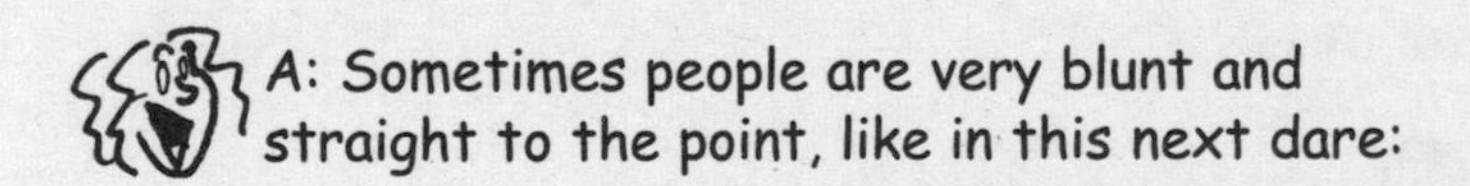

A: Sometimes people are very blunt and straight to the point, like in this next dare:

Get your penis pierced!!
Amy, Ballymun; Fiona Mc, Limerick; Emma, Dublin

Get a Prince Albert each, I double dare ya. Oh, and have a nice day! :-)
Darren, Carlow

WAX ATTACK

I dare ya to get a Brazilian wax EACH!
Ann, Cork; Diddy, Wexford; Rory, Galway & Conal

I dare ya to get both your legs waxed from hip to ankle. Do NOT bite down on anything while you are getting it done!
Deirdre, Kilkenny

I dare ya to get a full body wax!
Stephen, Kerry

Andrew, cut your hair and I suppose Damo could get his face waxed?
Barnes, Dublin

I dare ya to get your chest, legs and armpits waxed.
Donna, Kildare

BACK, SACK AND CRACK

A back, sack and crack wax. Nuff said.
Ryan, Derry

Get a back, sack and crack wax! See what us ladies have to go through... ;-)
Rachel & Karen, Una, Cebbie; Lollie, Westmeath; Danielle, Kinnegad

D: So are you saying you've got sacks?

A: We decided we would get our chests waxed and also a Back, Sack and Crack wax that everyone seemed so intent on us experiencing

We headed down to a waxing studio on Camden Street in Dublin and had a brief chat with the two lovely ladies who would be carrying out our procedure. To be honest we weren't that worried. I mean, if women can do it, then how hard can it be?

We stripped off our gear and lay down on our backs on the table and braced ourselves. What I didn't expect was the nice sensation of hot wax on my chest. I was lying there thinking: "You know what? This isn't too bad... in fact, it's quite nice..." Then BAM!!!! More pain than I could ever imagine as the wax lady ripped a massive clump of hair right from just above my left nipple. She hadn't even warned me or told me it would be fine. Without even waiting to see if I was ok, she ripped another clump right off! Blood was beginning to seep out of where my hair used to be.

To make matters worse Damo had already finished as he had a total of about 11 hairs on his chest. So as a result of his waxer having nothing to do, she decided she would help out with my stupid rug! Let me tell you this, I have never experienced anything more painful in the world than two people ripping and pulling hair off my torso.

Finally, after about 15 minutes, it was all done and I was able to see bare skin on my chest for the first time in about ten years. It was at this point that we realised, back...sack...crack...Hang on. Why'd we get our chest done!? That isn't even part of the dare!! All that pain and we hadn't even started yet!

We had a brief rest but not for long as we had to carry out the dreaded BSC. I decided to go with the classic 'lie on the front' position whereas Damo opted for the 'lie on the back and lift your legs as high possible with your ass pointed at the sky' position. They began applying the hot wax to our nether regions. Then without so much as a 'how's your mother' began ripping away like they were trimming hedges in an overgrown garden. Ripping, tearing, pulling, shredding... all this activity resulted in us feeling like we were on fire down there, and not from some weird STI. Finally it was all over and had apparently only lasted two and a half minutes. It seemed like a lifetime.

It's not until your hair's gone that you realise how much faster you can walk and that crack wax has cut minutes off bum wiping time. So there are good reasons to get it done, I mean, apart from that sexy swollen and bleeding look.

Thanks for the dare everyone.

DON'T MAKE FUN OF THE HOMELESS

The dares in this chapter are in very bad taste so be warned. Although there is a small chapter's worth so there must be a lot of sickos out there.

I dare ya to go up to the dirtiest homeless person you can find and lick the bottom of their foot.
Saranne

Go up to a group of drunk homeless men on the street, and say: "Dad! Dad! Is that you? I haven't seen you for 20 years!" It'll be worth it if one of them replies: "Son?"
Ciaran, Cavan

Go around asking for money loans from the homeless.
Sam, Dublin

Dress up as a homeless person and when someone gives you money, stand up and give them a hug. Say: "You're the kindest person in the world". Then try to kiss them.
Lisa, Dublin

I dare ya to dress up as a homeless person and go round shops in Dublin and wash their windows with dirty water.
Marty, Dublin

Dress up as homeless dudes with cardboard boxes and at a certain time, have a limo come pick you up from the spot where you were begging. Have the driver drape an overcoat over your shoulders and open the door for you.
Eric

A: I bet that's how James Brown would busk, ya know that...

I dare one of you to dress up as a homeless person and the other to wear a nice suit (aka a rich man in a suit). The 'rich' man robs the 'homeless' guy but then the 'homeless' guy chases after the 'rich' man to the disgrace of the public. It would be mad funny.
Anthony

I dare ya to ask a homeless person for €20.
Cian, Dublin & Sam, Dublin

Walk around town in old worn clothes with a sign that says: 'Will strip for food'. Approach lots of young fellas.
Adam , Crumlin

Give a homeless person €5 and ask for €2 change.
Lisa, Dublin

I dare ya to pretend to be a hobo and fall asleep in a restaurant on a table.
Kevin, Dublin

Dress up like a homeless person and walk into nice office buildings in the middle of the work day. Start washing people's windows in their offices for tips. (Like people wash car windshields at a stop light.) If security keeps stopping you, ditch the homeless outfit for a general service industry uniform and try again.
Adam, Dublin

Sit down as a beggar, but in brand new clothes, on a well-known street and see how much money you can get...
Micheal, Limerick

I dare ya to dress as hobos and go into all the fast food restaurants on Grafton Street and see which one lets you stay the longest (don't forget your vodka).
Michael, Kildare

D: We didn't do any of the homeless dares but if this comedy thing doesn't work out and Andrew and I end up on the streets, we'll give them a good hard go. We won't forget the vodka.

BACK ON THE STREETS

OFF THE CURB

Howdy chaps, I dare ya to run the length of the Port Tunnel as if you are running from disaster, dressed as plumbers!
Eric, Ballymun

Walk around town during rush hour, stop cars and hand out flyers to the drivers saying: "Hate to be stuck in traffic right now".
Paul, Clontarf

I dare ya to have a picnic on top of someone's car.
Hamza, Dublin

Touch as many builder's bums as possible in two hours.
Aine, Cork

Offer to valet park people's cars outside some of Dublin's shadier establishments.
Conor, Balrothery

I dare ya to hijack a horse and cart from the tinkers around Dublin city.
Billy, Dublin

D: That'd be great if they started chasing us in another horse and cart. "Follow dat horse!"

I dare ya to get some randomer's car and connect the horn to the brakes so that every time they brake the horn sounds.
Keith, Sligo

Strap Damo to the roof of a car and drive really fast.
Patrick, Roscommon

D: Ha! We attempted this on Andrew's new car and dented the roof in!! Hahaha!!

I dare ya to cycle go-karts around busy Dublin city centre.
Brendan, Offaly & Niall, Cork

I dare ya to go into a car sales garage and get into one of the cars that you're allowed to get into. Then start pretending to drive it like a child as loudly as you can.
Brendan, Dublin

I dare ya to drop a small child-like dummy out of a tree as a car drives under it.
Jonny, Co Monaghan

D: Remind me never to leave my child-like dummies in the care of Jonny.

Put a flash camera (using a Remote Flash Cord or something like that!) on top of one of the Garda speed cameras some night (ie when it's dark) and flash all the cars that go past, even the slow ones! They'll all think they've gotten tickets!
Mark, Dublin

I dare ya to get knocked down!
Shane, Cork

Try to knock unsuspecting cyclists off their bikes using a high-powered water gun from a car.
Rob, Co Limerick

Annoy Ray Darcy as much as possible while he is using the cycle lane on his way to work.
Patrick, Co Galway

I dare ya to have a jousting match, kitted out in full body armour, on bicycles in the middle of Grafton Street.
James, Dublin

Ride around a roundabout on a motorbike until ye get dizzy and fall off!
Damo, Kerry

Stage a fake 'knock down' in a busy area, with someone pretending to be knocked down and the other driving off laughing hysterically.
James, Co Tipperary

I dare ya to get tarred and feathered in the nude and cycle from Stillorgan to Dublin city. Once in the city lock your bike and sit down to a fry in a café.
Barry

I dare ya to ride on a 'Rideonlawnmower' up the M50. It would be the FUNNIEST THING EVER!
Stephen, Meath

Play Frogger extreme!! Jump across O'Connell Bridge in a frog suit! If any one asks you, you're Kermit the frog...
Katie

A: For anyone who doesn't know what Frogger is, it's a really old computer game where, and I'm not joking here, you played a frog who had to cross a busy street by bouncing. Seriously. That was it. Who needs Wii and Playstation 3 when you have games like that for slow, simple folk...

D: I used to love 'Frogger'!

A: Exactly

I dare you to play leap frog with anyone who is in the middle of tying their lace.
Linda, Dublin

Lie out in the middle of a busy street anywhere in Ireland and sing: "We shall, we shall NOT be moved!"
Mark, Mallow, Co Cork

I dare ya to paint out yellow no parking lines on streets in Dublin...
Dave

Stand at opposite ends of a pedestrian crossing, and when crossing the road start a fight with each other in front of the cars.
Jason, Limerick

Dress up as superheroes and supervillians and fight on the streets.
David

To leave a note on a TD's car saying 'Sorry I hit your car' and leave some other TD's phone number on the note.
Jude, Dublin

I got a parking ticket today and would just like to see what the parking attendant would do if you had no wipers. Yes, I dare ya to get a parking ticket on a car with no wipers.
Kraig, Kildare

D: Some people email us to vent. Well Kraig mate, I think you'll like Tim's dare...

Shoot a traffic warden. Two if you have time.
Tim

CLAMPING THE CLAMPERS

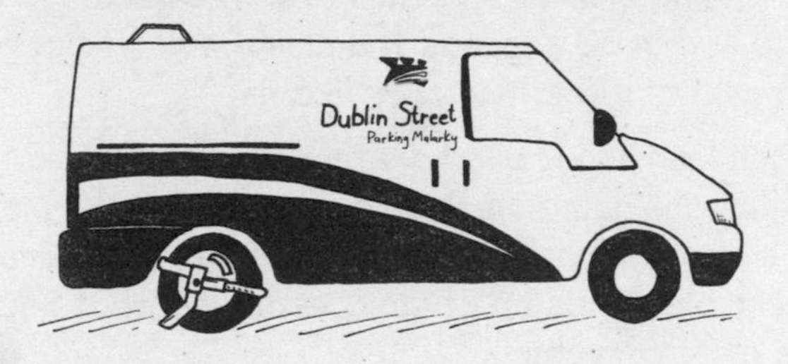

I dare ya to clamp the clampers!
Milie, Dublin; Stephen Lusk

A: Finally we get to do one of the things that everyone in the world wants to do - get revenge on one of the stupidest systems of traffic management in this day and age. It is surprisingly easy to get your hands on a clamp in hardware shops for a cheap, cheap, cheap price. We popped down, picked one up and then set off for the location of our ambush beside Fitzwilliam Square in Dublin.

We had arranged a car to be parked illegally and rang up the clamping department to tell them that they were blocking some spaces. They assured us they would be there ASAP so we went to our hiding spot and waited.

And waited. And then waited a bit more. Just while we think about it, if you are going to park illegally, feel safe in the knowledge that you have approx. 2 hours before the clampers arrive because that's how long they took to get to us even though we gave them the specific location.

Anyway, back to the point at hand, they finally arrived and we kept our eagle eyes on them, waiting for the perfect moment to pounce. They wandered off looking for victims and when they got far enough away from their van we got ready to make the move. We slunk over to the van and primed the clamp for the greatest feat ever and within 30 seconds the clamp was on and we were away! Let's see how *they* like it!

We began lounging around pretending that we didn't know what was going on. People started to take pictures of the clamped clampers. Finally they returned from their terrible deeds on other cars to see what had become of their vehicle.

Immediately they were confused and looking around for suspicious characters who might have carried out the deed. Of course we didn't look suspicious now having a rolled up black bin bag scrunched under my arm when it previously had something in it. Einstein was not needed to work out that equation. But they couldn't prove anything as nobody was about to rat out two clamp mavericks such as us.

The clamper guys began radioing into their head office to try to get someone out to help them out. As they were walking around looking confused, suspicious and curious they walked far enough away that we realised we could mess with their heads a bit more.

Their cavalry arrived in the form of a tow truck. So just when the two clamper guys got out of eyesight again to confer with their backup, we pounced back in and removed the clamp before you could say: "That's an €80 fine please." We retreated to the safety of another car where we dumped the incriminating evidence. We then began to wander back around towards the van to see now two even more confused clampers and their sceptical tow truck mates. You could actually see them wondering if it ever really happened.

Ah the joys of I Dare Ya.

We would also like to point out that you can easily purchase those clamps at many shops. If you already have four clamps on your car then you will never get clamped. We aren't saying you should do this, we are just letting you know.

WOOOO, DODGY

I dare ya to go into a Protestant pub on Sandy Row in East Belfast wearing a Celtic jersey. Offer someone a pint.

Rohan, Co Armagh

SPOT THE DIFFERENCE

Begin a military coup to take over Tory Island, Co Donegal, or any other island and declare it a free republic.
Jack

I dare ya to walk down the Shankill Road, Belfast (not Dublin) and say to as many people as possible: "Top of the morning to ya".
Jonnie, Belfast

Dress as Orangemen and march down Garvaghy Road in Portadown! Get the riot gear ready, good luck lads!
Garry, Derry

I dare ya to go up North wearing a balaclava and Celtic jerseys, singing Irish rebel songs and see how many petrol bombs get thrown at you.
Leon, Dublin

I dare ya to go to Dundalk and wear shirts that say I.R.A. RULES. See how long you last.
Gavin, Louth

Walk through the rough ends of Finglas holding hands.
Michael, Finglas

I dare yiz to march down Sheriff Street with a bowler hat and an orange sash beating a drum to the tune of The Sash.
Rob, North East Dublin

Walk through main street Finglas doing an Orange march.
Paul, Ballymun

I dare ya to stage a peaceful coup at the GPO and read out your own declaration of independence.
Darren, Belfast

I dare ya to go screaming down the streets of Dublin shouting: "RUN, RUN, WE'RE AT WAR WITH THE BRITISH!"
Fred

I dare you both to sing *God Save the Queen* together in Irish while wearing England football shirts out in any public street.
Brendan, Kilkenny

D: I remember the protests about playing *God Save the Queen* when Croke Park historically opened its gates to the English rugby team (when Ireland beat them 43-13!) in February 2007. It turned out to be a very moving moment indeed. Although if they had wanted to stop any threat of protests they could have played the Coronation Street theme as the English anthem instead. I think everyone would have been happy with that.

I dare ya to go around Dublin in camouflage clothes and recruit people to the IRA.
Gavin

A: Well that's good Gav, but surely if we were in camouflage gear then nobody would be able to see us.

Go to Limerick City and find crowded places. Shout: skangers, knackers, travellers and chavs.
Sean, Thurles

Go to the North Side of Cork (eg Knocknaheeny, Parklands, Fairhill) and have some conversations with locals. Try and use their lingo by using as many of the following words as possible: Beoir = Girl, Feen = Lad, Fla = Hot/Good Looking, Story Kid = Hello, Pavee = Traveller and whatever other words ye can think of that are used in Cork!

Rachel, Co Cork

D: Good dare Rachel and very informative about the culture!

In your best British accent I dare ya to proudly declare how better the English are than the Irish from the roof of your Union Jack painted car, while just in your Union Jack underpants!! This will cause a bit of a stir! Good luck lads!

Susan, Cork City

I dare ya to sell random junk (empty wine bottles, middle of toilet rolls, completed crosswords, etc) on Grafton Street. Tell people: "These will give your home a unique, modern lived-in feel."

Muireann, Castleknock

TERRY WRIST

I dare ya to walk around Dublin city centre dressed as Osama Bin Laden. Have a pair of handcuffs on your wrist attached to a briefcase and start roaring out gibberish.

Colm, Athlone

TRAVELLERS

I dare ya to enter a halting site and try to sell them a set of gates or carpets!!
Tim, Wexford

Come down to Tralee and go into an estate where travellers live. Dress like a traveller and try to start a fight with one of the travellers.
Conor, Kerry

I dare ya to go out and tell a farmer in his field to hurry up and harvest his crop cos there's a traveller's convoy on their way from Limerick. Tell him you've decided on this field to have ready for their arrival tomorrow. If you don't have it ready you'll be shunned from the family and you'd hate to see them come all the way from Limerick to live at the side of the road... howaya boss!
Gerry, Co Dublin

I dare ya to go to a traveller's halting site and pretend that you bought a second hand drill off one of the travellers the previous week. Complain that the drill doesn't work and you want your money back or a credit note.
Mark, Waterford

I dare ye to park a caravan at a halting site and pretend to be Australian tourists and that ye think that the halting site is a caravan park/tourist area. Don't forget to bring your deck chairs and mix with the locals!

Steve, Galway & Sheena, Wicklow

A: And if you like that one, something similar...

Spend the night on a traveller's site. Arrive with your own flash, silver/gold mobile home pulled along with your eco-friendly 4X4. Dress in Pringle clothing and mix with the locals. Have a BBQ, drinks, fist-fight etc.

Mr Riley, Knock

D: I can see why Mr Riley doesn't want to use his first name.

I dare ya to dress up and talk like travellers and go into five main car dealerships. Try and convince them to give you cleaning contracts with the company. (You will have to bring a mangy mop and bucket.) You have to stay in each dealership for a maximum time of 10 minutes (talking to staff about the cleaning contract).

Eve, Cork

MEAN...BUT FUNNY

Hide in an auld one's wheelie bin and when she comes to get it, frighten the sh*t out of her.

Michael Bin

Walk up to someone who is fat, poke their stomach and say: "Wow, you're a really big man".

Denis, Cork

Play the tuba 'with skill' while following overweight people around the place.
Karol

D: Even if you don't have the 'skill', give it a go. You'll still get bashed (or eaten).

I dare ya to steal different people's umbrellas and run away shouting: "Run, loser, run!!"
Deanie, Laois

I dare ya to carry around some English pounds and offer people a pound. If they say yes... hit them on the shoulder and run off!
Stevie, Cork

I dare ya to buy a toy gun and try to hold up someone in the street.
Mike, Enniscorthy

I dare ya to set up a bed for people to test, only for it to be wafer thin and anyone who lies on it will fall into a pool of water (or any other such substance, maybe beans or Dublin Bay sludge).
Karl, Santry

Light someone's newspaper on fire as they are reading it.
Dermot, Greystones

I dare ya to get on top of a building and drop water balloons on random people.
Sean, Co Dublin

I dare ya to go around town tying people up, either with sellotape or rope, and run off leaving them stranded.
Alan, Ballyfermot

Go to a small street and place a sign saying 'dodge ball game in action'. Then if someone walks past, clobber them with your balls.
Olan

D: We picked this one because we love the phrase 'clobber them with your balls'.

HUNKY MANKINIS

I dare the lads to wear one of those hunky 'mankinis' and go sunbathing on the boardwalk along the Liffey. And not the cleaner one – the one where the junkies hang out.
John Paul Larrigan

D: Thank you Borat. We did this dare and it appeared on the TV show. We were quite nervous about this dare. There's something about being almost nude in public which makes you feel so vulnerable. The upside is it looks very funny and should be recognised as a joke immediately... but you never know beforehand just what will happen.

We ordered two fluorescent green 'mankini' swimsuits off the internet, where else? It's quite invigorating waking up in the morning knowing that later that day you'll be sporting one of these for all to see. I'd recommend it to anyone. Although sleeping in and not doing the dare at all did seem like the saner option.

Andrew and I met the crew in the alleyway behind Arlington's pub. It was the only day it rained while filming for the telly. Typical, the one day we have to strip off. I knew I was going to freeze my nads off! Then what will the green latex stretch around? To make matters all the more awkward, we didn't have them on under our clothes so we had to change into them. There's nothing dodgy about that at all, stripping off while shady looking alley characters amble by looking you up and down. How do you explain your way through that? "It's for TV" is a bit pretentious. "We've got a spare, would you like to join us?" worked a lot better.

We used double-sided tape around the private areas to keep it in place. Thanks to the recent back, sack and crack wax dare it was a smooth hairless surface for applying adhesives. So there is a positive to getting your pubes ripped out by a stranger. We also used nut cups to protect our fellas and to hold us in. We looked hideous enough without having any extra surprises springing out.

So we were kitted up and ready to go. We stood on the cobblestones in our shoes and socks (bare feet wouldn't be a smart thing to do, plus for some reason it looked funnier) and nothing else except what appeared like a bright, thin 'V' drawn on the front and back of us. Mankinis look like normal thongs but someone's given you an atomic wedgie... and are just about as comfortable. How much naked skin we were baring became apparent when we could feel the elements of wind and a light misty rain in places we didn't know we had places. Andrew shoved his dark red (see Andrew? I didn't say 'red') head of hair into a tight black swim cap.

Carrying a beach towel, a bucket and spade, and two folding chairs with drink holders, we strutted down onto Bachelors' Walk along the Quays. The camera crew stayed close behind us (all the while doing close-ups of our behinds). As soon as we were on the roadside the horns started honking and people started yelling out. Confused stares burned in our direction. Now we know how women feel everyday of their lives. All that attention, it's horrible, isn't it ladies? Actually, we were thoroughly enjoying it. In fact, I smell a business venture. If you feel like you need a confidence boost, you should be able to hire a team to follow you around town throwing compliments your way. I can see it now...

Hey there! Want to know what it feels like to be the sexiest and most sought after person in the city? WELL NOW YOU CAN!! Call Sleazebags R Us and we send out our noisy and highly qualified team to make you and the world know just how great you are! We use techniques from leaning out car windows, hanging over balconies and scaffolding to simply walking past. As you go about your day you can hear such pleasantries as: 'Wooo Wooo, looking good girlfriend!!' 'Hey mate have you been working out?' 'Excuse me! Sexy people aren't allowed in here!' 'HONK HONK!!

Warrreuraaaggghhhl!!' 'Show us your tits!' and many more! Feel as beautiful, important and hassled as the sexiest of celebrities without the stress of actually getting famous! Sleazebags R Us - we put the Ease into Sleaze.

We shimmied in between slow moving cars and buses to get to the boardwalk while wolf whistles followed our every step. 'Wolf' refers to the kind of guy who gives unwelcome gestures to women but for years I wondered why it was called wolf whistling. As far as I was aware, no member of the dog family can whistle, although they can pant and drool, which I have to say I've been guilty of doing to women in public. The court case is next week.

We both strutted along the boardwalk. We passed people sitting on the bench enjoying the gluggy tide of the Liffey until we stepped into view. We opened up our folding chairs. Andrew sprawled along the deck after a quick slap of sunscreen. Yes, UV rays can penetrate clouds. We were relaxing there, just minding our own business when a uniformed guard marches up to ruin our holiday. As our doodles were covered we couldn't be arrested for indecent exposure so Mr Plod had to use a different tactic. "Right lads, you're causing an obstruction, seats on the boardwalk. I'm directing you to leave the area now under section 8 of the criminal justice order." And he kept going! "Failure to follow that direction constitutes an offence, the penalty of which can be a fine of up to €625 and/or a term of imprisonment of up to six months."

Full on! He knows his stuff. Imprisonment of up to 6 months!

"What are you in for?"

"Manslaughter, you?"

"Wearing this!" as you rip off your prison attire, jump up and start gyrating on the steel lunch table.

Then it got better.

"Can I swim in the river?" Andrew asked.

The Garda snaps back: "May I swim would be the correct way to ask it. I don't know if you can swim."

Wow, not only does he know his criminal justice orders but grammar as well. Who is this police machine? In case he started correcting other facets of our speech we hightailed it outta there, with a detour down O'Connell Street of course. All dressed up for town, why waste it?

When we put our clothes on back in the alley (hope no one started reading this book with that sentence) we kept the mankinis on underneath which gave us smirks on our faces for the rest of the day. Knowing at anytime you can go: "Give to Concern? How about I give this?!" Strip off and start hip thrusting people holding clipboards.

COUNTY BY COUNTY BEST OF

ANTRIM

I dare ya to pretend you are doing a survey on people, and ask randomers: What are your views on the discombobulation of humans? Do you think I'm discombobulated? I think you might be discombobulated. Tell them about the rate of discombobulation in the country... (Yeah I know this is sh*t, but I just love that word sooo much... even though I don't know what the word means... it is just the funniest word out there!)
Aileen, Antrim

ARMAGH

I dare ya to go to a really remote area, maybe about an hour and a half away from Dublin. Call a taxi firm from Dublin and ask them to pick you up. When they arrive, tell them you don't need to be picked up after all. They should be really pissed.
Mark, Co Armagh

Go to Sandy Row in Belfast and ask people walking along the street to become members of the Catholic Church.
Tommy, Co Armagh

CARLOW

Lads, I dare ya to go to a nicely packed Sunday Mass somewhere in the country (anywhere will do). Talk really loudly to each other during the Mass. When it's time for communion, go up and get the communion but then pretend to choke on it! See how that goes down!

Roisin, Co Carlow

Kiss each other.

Frankie, Carlow

CAVAN

I dare ya to jump into all of the 365 lakes in Cavan in 12 hours.

Brendan, Cavan

I dare ya to deliver a huge triple chocolate cake to Mary Harney.

Joyce, Cavan

Go into a female lingerie shop and ask the assistant for advice on what to buy for your girlfriend. When they ask what size she is, proceed to take out a blow up doll from your bag. Inflate it in front of them and say: "Do you wanna measure her yourself?" Feel free to improvise!!

Fergal, Cavan

Walk down Grafton Street dressed as professionally as possible. Start dancing randomly outside each shop that you can hear music coming from. Then just walk away normally and start again as soon as you hear more music.

John, Cavan

CLARE

Dress Andrew as a baby and push him down Grafton Street in a buggy on a Saturday afternoon. Take him out and burp him halfway down the street. Good luck lads.

James, Clare

I dare ya to go into a pet shop and ask how much it is to rent a sheep for an hour.

Michael, Co Clare

I dare ya to go into a coffee shop and order a cup of tea. When your tea is served, tell the waiter that you ordered coffee. When the waiter comes out with the coffee, say that you ordered tea and ask to see the manager. When the waitress goes to get the manager, leave the shop without the waitress or manager noticing...

Karl, Co Clare

CORK

Walk onto a golf course and wait until someone tees off. Then take their second shot for them and ask: "What do ya think of that?"

Eamon, Cork

Burst through church doors during a wedding ceremony and announce your love for the (random) bride to be!

Chris G, Cork

DERRY

I dare ya to go out onto the streets of Dublin and preach about a new and made up religion. You can make up the religion yourselves as I have neither the time, patience nor comic skill.

Kevin, Londonderry

I dare ya to go to a very busy car park, ie Liffey Valley, at a very busy time and every time a space becomes available and someone is waiting to get into it, cycle a bike into the space and walk away... just to drive them mad!
Frank, Co Derry

DONEGAL

Go into a cinema with video recording equipment and have t-shirts saying piracy creates jobs.
Foggymaster, Donegal

I dare ya to go into a newsagent on O'Connell Street and buy a lotto ticket on a Thursday with Wednesday's numbers. Then ask for Wednesday's numbers and demand your money, ya never know, they might pay out!
Michael, Donegal

Your dare is to walk into a supermarket that has a deli, for a ham salad (with mayonnaise) sandwich, BUT... instead of asking for one to be made up, walk around the supermarket and make it yourself. Open a loaf of bread and take out two slices. Open a mayonnaise jar, a packet of ham etc. When the sandwich is made, go up to pay and ask for a discount as you made it yourself.
Mary, Co Donegal

DOWN

I dare ya to streak across the pitch in Croke Park during a big match.
Ciaran, Down

Hand out brown envelopes (Christmas bonuses) to TD's outside the Dail – wearing Bertie masks if possible.
Stephen, Newry, Co Down

DUBLIN

Go sunbathing on O'Connell Street or on Grafton Street, like you're on the beach. Ask people passing by on the street to rub sun cream on your backs and play games like beach smash ball and beach volleyball. You both must also wear speedos or swimming trunks and sun shades.

Denis, Co Dublin

FERMANAGH

We didn't receive any dares from Fermanagh!

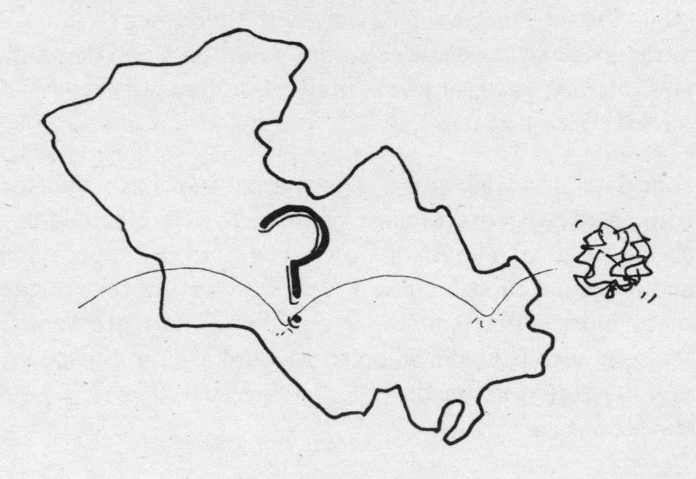

GALWAY

Put a large stick inside your pants and walk around the street acting as if you have a boner. You're sure to get strange looks!!

Diarmaid G, Galway

I dare ya to stand outside Thomond Park before a Munster game. Try to get them to sign a petition saying Leinster are a better team and that the 1978 Munster team that beat the All Blacks were on steroids.
Philly, Galway

Pretend you have narcolepsy and fall asleep on top of people, in furniture shops, in front of ATM's, in the middle of zebra crossings etc.
Shan, Galway

KERRY

I dare ye to come to Tralee, wait until all the schools are out for lunch, get naked and run around the Square and shout: "I'm a war-mongering latent homosexual!" Or pretend to be utterly rotten and go around asking random aul ones for money for more drink... or condoms... or even a pack of bananas! Make sure it's something odd and random like that!
Mandy, Tralee, Co Kerry

Go into a maternity ward in a hospital as a gay couple and start choosing which baby to bring home!! (Maybe ask a nurse for help.)
Roughmog, Co Kerry

During the Rose of Tralee festival, dress up as Roses – Dublin and Aussie Roses – and have your own float in the parade. Sign autographs for kids along the street afterwards. Try your best to get into places free saying you are Roses!! Even get Ray Darcy to accompany you to make it more real!
Olivia, Tralee, Co Kerry

I dare ya to walk up to someone on the phone, take the phone off them and start talking to whoever's on the other end.

Daragh, Co Kerry

KILDARE

To enter X Factor/You're a Star as a mute entrant.

Jack, Kildare

I dare ya to drive down the wrong way on the M50... blindfolded.

Don, Kildare

Lads, I dare ya to inflate condoms with helium, use a marker to decorate them as cartoon characters. Try to sell them to parents at an incredibly high price while dressed as nuns.

Conor, Kilcullen, Kildare

Pretend to be blind. Have the shades, a stick and a dog and ask people for directions. Once they have poured their hearts out trying to help, slide the shades down and thank them while looking them straight in the eyes.

Donna, Kildare

KILKENNY

Walk down Grafton Street on a busy day with a monkey.

David, Co Kilkenny

I dare Damo to go up to Andrew's mother and ask her out on a date.

Brendan, Kilkenny

Run out nude live on *The Late Late Show*. That would be better entertainment than that bore. Don't be shy lads.... you can do this for IRELAND!!
Eymard, Kilkenny

LAOIS

I dare both of you to go paintballing with 10 army rangers... and you're naked!!!
Ollie, Laois

Go into a secondary school, walk into a classroom and tell the teacher that you're after being sent from the department to teach. Take over the class in front of the teacher.
Siobhan, Laois

I dare ya to go to a crowded place and when some random person walks by, start roaring at the top of your voice: "I'm not interested in you. There are plenty more fish in the sea, now leave me alone."
Dermot, Laois

LEITRIM

Knock on people's doors and walk into their kitchen and pour yourself a cup of tea. Then thank them and walk out again.
Robert, Co Leitrim

LIMERICK

I dare ya to go to a beach or seaside... come running out of the water and go up to somebody. Damo should ask them: "Is this Australia?" When they say no, one of you reply: "Feck it anyway, we must have taken a wrong turn." Then run back into the water and start swimming again!
Edel & Orla, Limerick

I dare ya to have a pellet gun fight in the middle of a busy area. Dress up in a tuxedo and act like James Bond as much as possible.

Patrick, Limerick

I dare ya to wear the Leinster rugby shirt, put on your best D4 accents and go to Thomond Park to see Munster play in the European Cup while lecturing everyone on why ye think Leinster are better!

Sean, Limerick City

To act like D4 rugby heads and hold a protest outside Croke Park with a banner that says: "We'd rather play in England than in this shithole"

Laura, Roisin & Niamh, Limerick

LONGFORD

I dare ya to come onto Mary Harney.

Paddy, Co Longford

LOUTH

I dare ya to give me the money that you earn from the show to spend on presents for me and my friends!

Gareth, Louth

MAYO

Go down Grafton Street in a wheelchair, suddenly fall out of the wheelchair and make a huge mess of it! Wait for a few people to come and help you and then jump up to your feet and shout: "I'm fixed, I can walk!" Then run down the street and keep shouting!

Iarla, Mayo

Try to chat up Eamon Dunphy at a bar. Try to land a sneaky kiss and ask for a phone number. Play it cool, get emotional if he rejects your advances. Then the other one of your duo will approach Dunphy and accuse him of hitting on your other half.
Cillian, Mayo

MEATH

I dare ya to walk directly and as close as possible behind a stranger without saying anything. If he/she turns around, you turn around and act like you're looking somewhere else. Follow them for as long as you can before they crack up...
Greg, Meath

Go up to a council worker digging up the roads and start filling back in the holes.
Margaret, Meath

Dress up in women's clothes and approach a group of men. Single one out and say: "You promised to call me, you promised it wasn't a one night stand."
Barbara, Meath

I dare ya to wear an Ireland jersey with Steve Staunton on the back of it. Try and start a petition to bring back Steve Staunton as Ireland manager and say stuff like 'he's the greatest' and all that...
Sean, Meath

MONAGHAN

I dare ya to come to Monaghan and start a 'Close the Hospital Down' campaign... if you're brave enough!!
Kevin, Co Monaghan

Well lads, I dare ya to go into a chemist looking a bit nervous! Tell one of the staff that you think you might have an STD and can you buy something for it! They will (in shock) tell you to go straight to your doctor or clinic for a check. After you have listened to their advice, ask the kind shop assistant out on a date! Mention you only think you have an STD and that they should be ok... you think. Or suggest that ye can both go to the clinic tomorrow! It will be epic!!

Stephen, Monaghan

OFFALY

Why not go speed dating and get attached to people who you meet there. Get upset about them seeing other people and break up with them just as the time is up.

Mark, Offaly

I dare ya to push a penny round a toilet bowl with just your tongue...

Sharon, Offaly

ROSCOMMON

Keep driving around a roundabout for five hours.

Damien, Roscommon

SLIGO

I dare ya to go up to random people in the street and ask them what sex they are and after they say it, laugh hysterically!!

Áine, Sligo

I dare ya to buy something in a shop but try to pay for it using one of those giant cheques.

Cathal, Sligo

TIPPERARY

Walk through one of the roughest estates in Ireland as a bible preacher!!

Emily, Tipperary

Wear the national English soccer jersey and a pair of Union Jack trousers to one of those college 'County Colours' nights out.

David, Tipperary

TYRONE

I dare ya to get into the back seat of a taxi through one door and just get out the other door straight away and ask: "How much do I owe ya?"

Josh, Co Tyrone

WATERFORD

Go to a busy Dublin street and wait to cross the road. But ask someone to hold your hand while crossing the street. Say that your mother usually does it for you and she won't let you cross the street on your own.

Jason, Waterford

I dare ye to eat loads and loads of fudge. Then with your mouths full of fudge try and shout: 'FUDGE.'

Jessie, Waterford

Dress up as leprechauns and run around the Square Shopping Centre in Tallaght looking for your pot of gold in shops, restaurants and in people's bags!

Kellie, Waterford

WESTMEATH

I dare Andrew to walk up and down Grafton Street holding Damian on a dog leash and a dog collar with Damian jumping and barking at other people. Make Andrew tie Damian around a pole while he goes into a shop on the street.

Gary, Westmeath

WEXFORD

I dare ya to go up to skangers on the streets of Dublin and ask them: "Would you like to star in a new show highlighting poverty in Ireland?"

Richard, Wexford

WICKLOW

I dare ya to go to a public place and every few seconds to strike a pose as though someone is taking your picture. Try to pose with statues and other people.

Ciara, Wicklow

Go into an Xtravison store with a large coke, popcorn and a fold up chair. Sit down and watch the movie they are showing in the store. Say to the customers and staff: "Be quiet, I'm trying to watch a movie."

Paul, Co Wicklow

32 COUNTIES IN 24 HOURS

D: It can be done!! Andrew and I did 30 counties in 24 hours without speeding. Another 30 minutes and we would've made it to Monaghan and Meath which were the two we missed. We spent 40 minutes at Tony's Takeaway in New Ross, Co Wexford so if we got the food to 'take away' as the name suggests, we would've made it.

Also we drove the I Dare Ya-mobile (jade green Fiat Punto) around Ireland clockwise, which is the outside lane. If we went around the opposite way, similar rule to a race track, we'd be on the inside lane which would be slightly less the distance.

This was our favourite dare to carry out. It's a real adventure and race against time. Don't forget the caffeine, chewy sweets or chupa chups and for the other passengers benefit, don't eat baked beans prior to travelling.

JUST PLAIN NUTS

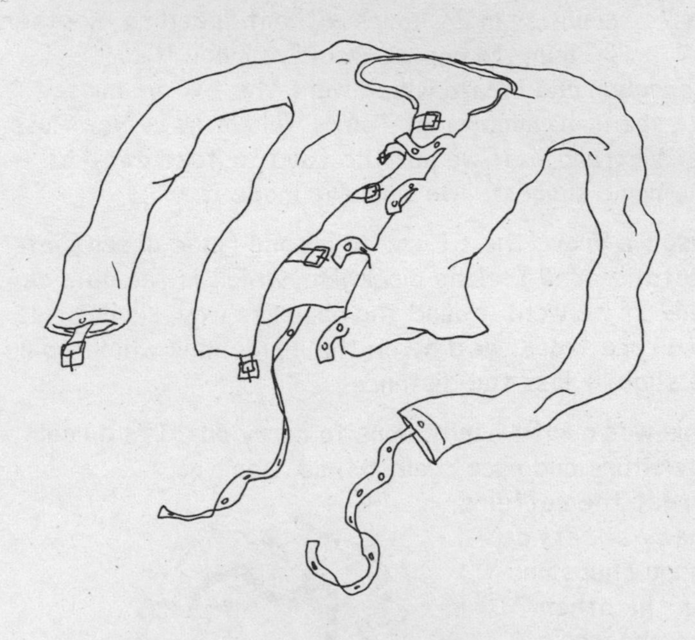

Ladies and gentlemen, it's now time for our favourite chapter. It's pretty random and yes, some of these people should be locked up in a padded cell.

I dare ya to fly.
Jack, Castlebar

I dare ya to get sex change operations.
Lez, Wicklow

Eat your own face.
Pat, Kerry

I dare ya to go to a local art gallery or a library and shout "DONKEY!" as loud as you can.
Josh & Billy, Co Tyrone

Stay up for five days.
Shane, Laois

Damo, I dare ya to ruin Andrew's week.
Rebecca

D: You got it!

Legally change your first names from Damian to 'Doctor Damian' and Andrew to 'Sir Andrew'. See how much stuff you can get away with by pretending to be a doctor and a knight.
Ciaran, Cavan

I dare ya both to get married to each other.
Michaela, Warrenpoint, NI

I dare ya to get a job in a crèche or playschool on 'work experience' and start fighting with the kids for their toys.
Sinead, Cork

I dare ya to go into a nursing home pretending to be nurses. Then strip in front of the old women and offer to free them from the home!!
Mark, Co Louth

DO SOMETHING CRAZY
Grace, Mayo

D: There's one thing we can say about Grace: she certainly has a big imagination.

I dare ya to jump off a bridge singing *Don't Stop Me Now* by Queen.
Aoife, Naas

Try to break the world record for the amount of hard boiled eggs ever eaten by one person.
Rob, Kilkenny

Get 16 year old girls to tell their parents they're pregnant and record their reaction!!
Amy, Galway

I dare ya to stand on a balcony of an apartment, hotel etc and throw buckets of ice cold water over random people.
Karen, Leixlip

Run around Roundwood in ragged clothes saying you escaped from Michael Jackson's house.
Mikey, Co Wicklow

Lick my balls please.
Kevin, Lusk

D: Well, Kevin did say 'please'.

I dare ya to go into a library and start shouting "BOGEYS".
Shane, Co Armagh

I dare ya to move into a show house for a night.
Anne-Sophie, Limerick

I dare both of you to spend the night in the haunted house past Oughterard in Co Galway on the Clifden Road. Ask anyone in the area and they will tell you the story.
Richard

D: Who ya gunna call...

Go on strike outside the bank.
Gerry, Limerick

I dare ya to give me €500!
Bryan, Wexford

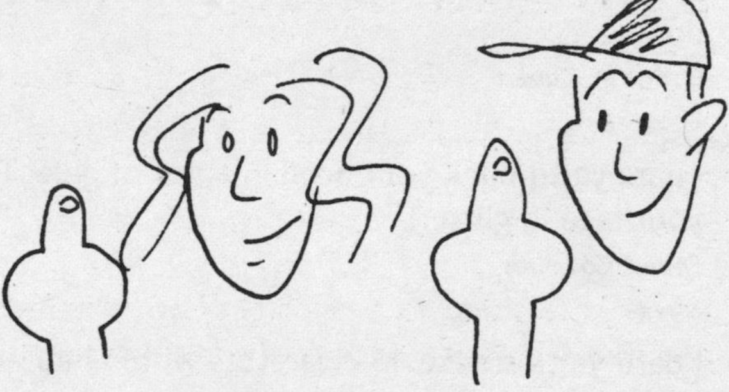

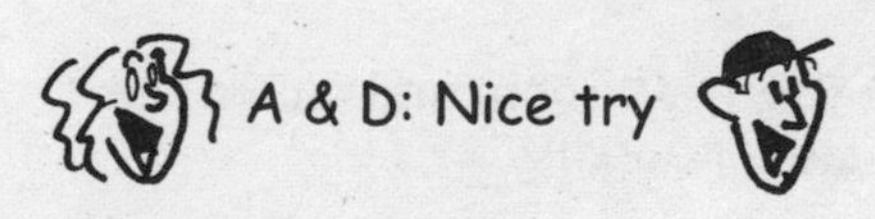

To sell a 'slave' on eBay.
James

I dare yous to ride each other!
Bill, Dublin

D: Ride each other!? Glenn puts it a little more poetically:

I dare ya to make love to each other.
Glenn, Portrush

Get a vasectomy.
Peadar, Aran Islands

I dare ya to go to a beauticians or hairdressers and start applying make-up and beauty products to waiting customers, acting as if you work there.
Jessica, Limerick

To stand on the roof of a hairdresser and pour water over the customers as they're coming out with their hair just done.
Donna M, Dublin

I dare ya to dunk your head in a pot of glue! Then cover your face in glitter!
Emma, Co Louth

I dare ya to smoke 15 cigarettes within half an hour...EACH!
Jennifer

I dare ya to break into the RTÉ news room and record the news while dressed up as Anne Doyle!!!
Aoife, Clonmel

I dare ya to shave every hair off your body.
Ciara, Tipperary

Go into a computer shop and ask can you be shown a computer. While they are telling you about it, take out a DVD of a movie and put it in and start watching it...
Sean, Co Galway

To go to a job interview in your pyjamas. (The job interview cannot be in Sheriff Street.)
Michael, Dublin

D: And now a dare for everyone who hates their job...

Tell your boss he's an ignorant asshole!
Shane, Sligo

D: Oh yeah, that'd be sweet...

A: Although technically we are own bosses so we would be telling ourselves that we were ignorant assholes...

D: I think I just fired myself.